LITTLE BOOK OF BIG IDEAS

Economics

First published in Great Britain in 2007

A & C Black Publishers Ltd
38 Soho Square
London W1D 3QZ
Tel: 020-7758 0200
Fax: 020-7758 0222
Web: www.acblack.com

Conceived and produced by
Elwin Street Limited
144 Liverpool Road
London N1 1LA
www.elwinstreet.com

Designer: Thomas Keenes
Illustrators: Richard Burgess, Emma Farrarons

A CIP catalogue record for this book is
available from the British Library.

ISBN-10: 0-7136-8337-6
ISBN-13: 978-0-7136-8337-0
Printed in China

LITTLE BOOK OF BIG IDEAS
Economics

Mathew Forstater
Introduction by Professor James Rollo

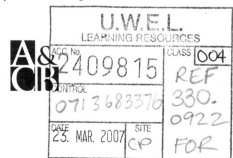

Contents

Historical and Institutional Economics

Development Economics

Introduction

Economics rules the modern world. From controlling inflation to understanding globalisation; from pricing your mobile phone call to pricing use of the motor car; from measuring poverty to measuring happiness; from liberalising trade to restricting pollution; from making war to building the peace, economists and economics are at the heart of the debate and at the heart of policy making.

On Wall Street, in London, Paris, Frankfurt, Tokyo, Shanghai, Sydney and Mumbai, economists sit at the centre of decision-making that determines the fate of your savings, the level of your pension, the future of your employer, indeed the fate of your government as they advise on buying and selling company shares, government bonds and currencies. By that measure alone economics is the most influential social science. Economists helped invent financial derivatives and thus brought hedge funds into being. It was one such hedge fund that brought about the collapse of sterling in 1992, which in turn led to the ruination of the UK government of John Major and made one man, George Soros, a billionaire. No other social science has, or even aspires to, a Nobel Prize, giving economics an equivalence of intellectual standing and influence with the physical sciences and medicine.

The most influential ideas of economists are contested from outside and inside the profession. And this is, perhaps, no surprise. The economy – the way in which human beings organise production, distribution, consumption and exchange of goods and services, and how the balance of consumption, investment prices, employment, and government expenditure are managed – is immensely complex. The key variable, human behaviour, is active not passive. Even apparently simple economies are hard to understand because people change their behaviour in response to changes in the information available to them.

The ideas of economists sometimes seem to stand common sense on its head. Since Adam Smith, most economists have taken as a given that opening up the national economy to foreign trade and investment is a good thing. Increased competition reduces prices to consumers and increases the efficiency of production. This same competition leads to inefficient domestic firms going out of business with consequent unemployment, so while the many may benefit a little, the few lose their livelihoods. The economist's answer is that unemployed resources should be redeployed to more efficient uses and in the long term the economy will be more competitive and incomes will be higher.

If unemployment is slow to clear then whole regions, cities and towns and individuals can face poverty for years and sometimes generations. In those circumstances it is often hard to credit the benefits of international trade.

As Keynes said, 'in the long run we are all dead'. That is why the emergence of the giant workforces of China and India onto the global stage raises such fears. It is also why it is important to grasp the concept of comparative advantage, which says that even an economy that is the most efficient producer of everything in the world would find it rational to concentrate on the products it is relatively most efficient at and leave those it is relatively least efficient at to the rest of the world. This means that everyone in the world has the possibility of a livelihood in a global economy.

Historically, some of the best minds have wrestled with the problem of how to understand the economy. These thinkers have developed a body of theory and evidence that, while incomplete, has made much of the modern world what it is. This book might be small but the ideas are big and their influence huge.

Professor James Rollo
University of Sussex

Aristotle

In his major work, *The Politics*, the philosopher Aristotle identified two types of productive and distributive activity of Ancient Greek society. One he called *œconomia*, and the other *chrematistiké*.

Born: 384 BCE, Macedonia, Greece
Importance: The first thinker on economic activity
Died: 322 BCE, Euboea, Greece

Œconomia, from which the word 'economics' is derived, literally means household management. It was associated with orderliness – regular, dependable pursuits, such as growing subsistence food and tending animals, or the craft work involved in the production of clothes, tools, and furniture, etc. (Curiously, Aristotle's definition of *œconomia* also included piracy as a means of making a living.)

Chrematistiké, on the other hand, concerns the making and lending of money, wealth accumulation, commerce, earnings and all those pursuits we now identify with economic activities. Perhaps the modern use of the word 'economics' is ironic, and given Aristotle's taxonomy, the discipline should be called chrematistics.

Ancient Greece was a varied society with the presence of both tyranny and democracy. Administratively, its territory was comprised of both the *polis* – cities – and the countryside. Its population was engaged in both agrarian subsistence production and inter-state trade. While Aristotle considered *œconomia* to be necessary for every society, he regarded chrematistics as dangerous and destructive to society due to its lack of limits on the activities involved.

Œconomia was considered a natural activity, whereas *chrematistiké* was not. And while Aristotle would favour the sphere of exchange as long as it was used to satisfy the natural requirements of a household, he was opposed to the sphere of exchange extending beyond that to what could be regarded as money-making. Aristotle detested usury, or earning interest on money. Making money out of money was considered unnatural. Aristotle believed that chrematistics and money-making were dangerous and destructive to society due to the lack of any limits on the activities involved.

'Of the art of acquisition then there is one kind which is natural and is part of the management of a household. […] There is another variety of the art of acquisition which is commonly and rightly called the art of making money, and has in fact suggested the notion that wealth and power have no limit….'

Aristotle, *The Politics*

In *The Nichomachean Ethics, Book V*, Aristotle recognised that exchange ratios have both a moral and analytical dimension. Money serves as a measure of value and a medium of exchange. It functions as a means of quantifying the comparable worth of goods. These issues were to be debated by scholars over the centuries to come.

As Karl Polanyi would later put it, Aristotle 'discovered the economy'. He identified the main focus of economics as the necessary distribution of material goods and services to permit ongoing social reproduction, and by what institution such distribution will be satisfied.

St Thomas Aquinas

St Thomas Aquinas is perhaps best known as a theologian, but his great thirteenth-century work *Summa Theologica* also examined questions of economics. Following in the tradition of Aristotle, he brought a moral dimension to economic analysis, stressing the need to do what was right over what would simply make money.

Born: 1225, Roccasecca, Italy
Importance: Moral philosopher on money, price and trade
Died: 1274, Fossaunuova, Italy

Between the fifth and ninth centuries CE there was an extraordinary absence of money, a virtual demonetisation, in Europe: most exchanges were carried out in kind. Under European feudalism serfs had to pay their lords for everything from the use of the mill for processing their grain to marrying off their children; this payment was not in monetary form, but as crops, labour and so on. However, from the ninth century onward Europe saw a gradual increase in mining and coinage, as more and more goods appeared for sale.

This led to the question of how to determine a fair price, since the period of demonetisation meant there was no prior monetary price to refer to. Aquinas addressed this and many other questions in his *Summa Theologica* (1266–1273), stating that a thing should not be sold for more than its 'just price'. To justify his viewpoint, Aquinas made arguments based on moral authority, rather than what would be considered today as *analysis*.

Question 77 in *Summa Theologica*, titled 'On Fraud Committed in Buying and Selling', is a fascinating series of investigations into the following questions:

1. Whether a man may lawfully sell a thing for more than it is worth.

2. Whether a sale is rendered unlawful by a defect in the thing sold.
3. Whether a seller is bound to point out the defect in a thing sold.
4. Whether in trading it is lawful to sell a thing for more than what was paid for it.

Aquinas' deliberations upon the first question, of whether it is lawful to sell a thing for more than it is worth, provide a good example of his way of thinking and his emphasis on moral rather than analytical arguments. Since justice in human exchanges is determined by civil law, it appears that it is lawful to sell a thing for more than it is worth. That which is common to all men seems to be natural and not sinful. If everyone accepts the maxim of 'buy cheap and sell dear', it seems to be lawful to sell a thing for more than it is worth and to buy a thing for less than it is worth. However, opposed to this is the Biblical maxim, 'Do unto others that which you would have them do unto you'. Thus, Aquinas concluded, it is wholly sinful to commit the fraud of selling a thing for more than its just price.

The same conclusion was deduced for Question 78 of *Summa Theologica*, 'On the Sin of Usury'. Receiving interest on loans would be considered unjust by Aquinas. The influence of Aristotle's economic philosophy can be seen in Aquinas's work; for example, Aquinas would also regard money as unnatural, since it did not grow by itself. This was another strong argument against earning interest on loans.

It is striking how so many activities that were once deemed immoral and even illegal later became not only acceptable, but were considered beneficial to society.

Ibn Khaldun

A Muslim philosopher, historian and statesman, Ibn Khaldun
was among the African travellers of the medieval Maghreb who
documented the social formations of northern and western Africa
and their economic connections to Europe and Asia. Khaldun was
a political economist of the Classical type, employing
an analysis that combined economics, sociology,
political science, history and moral philosophy.

Born: 1332, Tunis, Tunisia
Importance: The forerunner
of Classical political
economy
Died: 1405, Cairo, Egypt

His major work is *Al Muqaddimah*, or the
Introduction to History. While Khaldun is generally
recognised as the father of sociology, his contribution
to economics cannot be underestimated. It is striking
how Khaldun's ideas anticipated Classical
political economy.

Ibn Khaldun's theory of the life cycle of civilisations compared
society to a living organism that was subject to decline and death
as a universal cause. Periods of economic progress were
characterised by large-scale production based on the division and
specialisation of labour. Khaldun's analysis of the division of
labour is remarkably similar to that of Adam Smith in *The Wealth
of Nations*. Specialisation increases productivity and, as a result,
output rises above the subsistence level. But Khaldun analyzed the
nations of northern and western Africa as being based on a
surplus that was the result of long-distance trade rather than one
exacted from peasants. For centuries up until the European
discovery of the Americas, western Africa was the chief supplier
of gold to the Roman Empire, medieval Europe, the ancient East
and the Arab world. The African states of Almoravides and
Almohades in the north and Ghana, Mali and Songhai in the West
all had similar social structures according to Khaldun.

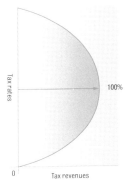

Tax rates

100%

0

Tax revenues

Left: The Laffer curve demonstrates how higher tax rates may result in lower tax revenue. At first, as tax rates rise, tax revenue rises; but at some point, the higher tax rates may discourage additional activity, resulting in lower tax revenues.

Khaldun also anticipated the notion of social cohesion arising from 'fellow-feeling' (or empathy) found in Adam Smith's *Theory of Moral Sentiments*. For Khaldun, 'group-feeling' enables the cooperative structure of social organisation. The stronger the sense of group solidarity, the more individuals are likely to adhere to the behaviours necessary for a well-functioning society.

A distinction between natural and social needs is prominent in Khaldun's analysis. Social needs arise due to economic progress and diversity of commodities at people's disposal. Affluence and the need for luxuries were associated with the mature stage of social development. As government strives for more wealth, it increases taxes. This would ultimately ruin the state as tax revenues would shrink due to citizens being discouraged to work or leaving the country. Some scholars find the analysis similar to later supply-side economics, with Khaldun making the essential argument, later known as the Laffer curve, where higher tax rates result in lower tax revenue.

Khaldun saw the economy as a self-regulating system, the key to all forms of economics. He recognised the price and profit mechanisms, the forces of supply and demand, the stimulating effect demand has on growth, as well as the existence of competition. Khaldun also wrote on various types of property rights, anticipating Locke's labour-determined theory of property.

Pre-Classical Economics

Thomas Mun

Mercantilism comes from the word 'merchant', which means 'trader'. The Mercantilist movement arose in Europe in the mid-sixteenth century, and remained potent until the middle of the eighteenth century. Thomas Mun was one of its most distinguished contributors of ideas and principles.

Born: 1571, London, England
Importance: The proponent of Mercantilist theories
Died: 1641, London, England

Trade, and in particular international trade, occupied a central place in Mercantilist principles. Mercantilists lived in a period of continuing trade expansion in Europe, with the proliferation of markets and the rise of the merchant class. Increased commercial activity made merchants very influential in European governments and public policy was formulated to reflect their views on trade and manufacturing.

Thomas Mun was one such merchant. From 1615 he served as the Director of the British East India Company, a huge, state-monopoly trading company. Mun expressed his ideas on foreign trade in his famous works *A Discourse of Trade from England unto the East Indies* (1621) and *England's Treasure by Foreign Trade* (1664), the latter being perhaps the most famous exposition of Mercantilist principles. Mun advocated a trade surplus, or the excess of exports over imports, as the means of increasing a nation's wealth.

The importing of cheap raw materials was encouraged since they would be used to manufacture expensive finished goods that would then be sold in exchange for gold and silver. The main idea was that the original outflow of gold and silver be less than its final inflow, and the maxim was to 'sell more than you buy' in order to increase the 'treasure' or wealth of a nation.

Mercantilists held a derogatory view of competition, and saw accumulation of hard money as the core of individual and national wealth and prosperity. The movement believed in state intervention, in particular to regulate foreign trade, to impose tariffs on imports and encourage the export of finished products, and would also grant patents of monopoly to domestic manufacturing companies.

However, the Mercantilists failed to recognise that accumulation of money through trade is not the same as wealth creation. A trade surplus for one country can result in a trade deficit for another, but Mercantilists did not see it this way. For them, international trade had to be a win–lose situation where the winning country held the surplus, and the losing country suffered a deficit.

While their approach was fallacious, Mercantilists should be granted credit for marking a sharp break from the Aristotelian and Scholastic approaches to economic issues. Since Mercantilists were shrewd businessmen and government officials, they engaged in little abstraction and were primarily interested in practical applications of their ideas through government policy.

Mercantilism: Holds that a nation's prosperity depends on its supply of capital, and that the global volume of trade is unchangeable. Therefore, the best way for a state to increase its amount of capital is to encourage a positive balance of trade with other nations, with low imports and high exports. This can be achieved by introducing tariffs to discourage foreign imports.

Pre-Classical Economics

John Locke

In his *Two Treatises of Government*, British political philosopher John Locke outlined two criteria for judgements: reason and revelation. In the case of reason, Locke argued, it is clear that all people have a right to subsist and a right to what nature provides for the preservation of life. In the case of revelation, scripture makes it clear that God gave all property to Mankind in common.

Born: 1632, Somerset, England
Importance: Theories on property and capital accumulation
Died: 1704, Essex, England

How then could anyone own property if that meant denying it to others? Locke responded that while God gave property to all in common, he also endowed humans with reason, and to make use of it. Therefore, there must be some way of appropriating the fruit. Further, while God gave the earth and animals in common to all people, every man has property in his own person. From this Locke concluded that one's own labour and the work of one's hands must be one's own.

The common property of nature becomes one's own when it is mixed with one's own labour. The apples you pick are yours, because your labour has been applied to them. As Locke stated, 'The labour that was mine, removing them out of that common state they were in, hath fixed my property in them'. And this property essentially means the right to deny use or access to anyone else.

Yet there should be limits to the amount of property accumulation permitted. One can enjoy as much as one can make use of before it spoils, since nothing was made by God for man to spoil or destroy. In the case of land, as much of it can be appropriated as property as a man can enclose by his labour, as long as there is enough left for everyone else. Therefore,

acquisitiveness is bounded by the limits of one's labour and by man's capacity to enjoy the good before it is spoiled. Locke goes further and states that the enclosing of land and application of labour to it does not lessen the amount left for others, but increases it to the extent that land is used for production.

Locke also indicated that if goods are given away or traded for something else before they spoil, then the goods are not wasted. If something does not spoil, it can be accumulated to any extent (within the limit set by one's own labour). Locke noticed that the invention of money gave people the opportunity to enlarge their possessions. Because it did not spoil, gold could be accumulated. He thus concludes, in paragraph 50 of *Two Treatises of Government*, as follows: 'it is plain that the consent of men have agreed to a disproportionate and unequal possession of the earth – I mean out of the bounds of society and compact; for in governments the laws regulate it; they having, by consent, found out and agreed in a way how a man may, rightfully and without injury, possess more than he himself can make use of by receiving gold and silver, which may continue long in a man's possession without decaying for the overplus, and agreeing those metals should have a value.'

Economics and the Economy

What is economics? Economics is the study of the economy. That just begs another question, not so easily answered: what is the economy? At a fundamental level, the economy concerns how societies organise themselves to provide for their material wellbeing. This primarily concerns the decisions that have to be made regarding production and distribution.

While all societies must have an economy, the study of the economy primarily concerns the study of a capitalist, or market-orientated, economy, rather than a planned economy. In earlier traditional or command societies, markets either were not present or were subsidiary to other ways of organising production and distribution. In traditional societies, the economy was embedded in what today would be perceived as cultural (or even ritual or religious) institutions. In command societies, the economy was embedded in political institutions, such as European feudalism or various forms of slave-based production systems. Only with the development of capitalism did the economy become 'disembedded'.

The rise of market-orientated economies introduced a specifically economic institution that determined production and distribution. With the onset of capitalism, questions were asked concerning the operation of market systems and the forces that might regulate such a system. Market systems are not perfect – there are booms and crashes, recessions and depressions, inflation and deflation, unemployment and financial crises – but neither are they completely random. Even economists who emphasised the problems with capitalism, such as Marx and Keynes, still viewed markets as self-regulating, ruled by some basic tendencies (or laws). There are different theories regarding these tendencies, including Mercantilist, Classical, Neoclassical (or Marginalist), Marxian, Keynesian and Institutionalist schools of economic thought, each with various sub-schools. But what these views all share is the idea that some regularities and reliable behaviours can be identified that give insight into the way the market works.

The philosopher Adam Smith, who was also one of the great classical political economists, wrote in his *History of Astronomy* that human beings feel a kind of anxiety from the unexpected and unfamiliar, and contentment from the familiar. So, we try to classify and categorise the world in order to make sense of it all. This, Smith says, is the purpose of philosophy, the purpose of theorising: to find the orderliness in the hubbub. This is all the more necessary and difficult because the object of study in this case – the capitalist economy – is not static, but dynamic, meaning that the rules that governed its operation at one period of time may no longer be active, and other regularities may have taken over. Therefore, any economic theory has to be considered within its historical context.

In addition, any explanation of capitalism's inner logic also affects public policy, which in turn affects our lives. Another British economist, G. L. S. Shackle, went so far as to say that whereas 'in natural science, what is thought is built upon what is seen, in economics what is seen is built upon what is thought'. How we interpret the economic activities that we observe in society, how we literally see them, is virtually determined by what others have thought (and written) about them – to a much greater extent than we might realise.

David Hume

As with many of the early writers on political economy, David Hume's ideas are found in the fields of philosophy and political theory as well as in economics. In Hume's *Political Discourses* (1752), he discussed issues pertaining to the balance of trade, commerce, money and interest, and made the distinction between wealth and money. He criticised the Mercantilist proposition that accumulation of specie – gold and silver – is the key to a nation's wealth. Instead, Hume measured wealth in terms of the stock of labour and the quantity of goods and services produced.

Born: 1711, Edinburgh, Scotland
Importance: Anti-mercantilist views on international trade
Died: 1776, Edinburgh, Scotland

Hume showed that foreign trade can be mutually beneficial for all countries, and that there is a built-in mechanism in an economy toward international equilibrium. That is, trade is a win–win situation and not win–lose as argued by the Mercantilist writers. Hume's 'price-specie flow mechanism' demonstrated the fallacy of the trade surplus approach advocated by the Mercantilists.

The key to 'price-specie flow mechanism' is to understand the Classical quantity theory of money, which relates the stock of money in an economy to the price level. That is, prices will rise in proportion to an increase in money supply and change the terms between trading nations. The Mercantilists, in contrast, did not consider this possibility. For them, money would have an effect only on the volume of trade; however, for Hume money was akin to oil, allowing the wheels of trade to roll more easily.

For example, two nations are engaged in trade with one another. Nation A runs a trade deficit, with an outflow of money to nation B. Nation B has a trade surplus equal to A's deficit, and therefore faces an inflow of money into its economy from nation A and so its prices will rise. Conversely, prices in nation A will fall due to its outflow of currency. The change in relative prices will alter the terms of trade between the countries against nation B, as its goods will become more expensive than the goods in the deficit country, nation A. Money will, as a consequence, flow from B to A. This continues until the value of exports equals the value of imports in both nations, and there is balanced trade between them. Hume demonstrated this argument with hard money – gold and silver. He used the term 'specie' to denote money, and hence 'price-specie flow mechanism', which argued that the economy has a built-in tendency toward international equilibrium. Any policies aimed at favourable balance of trade is therefore self-defeating.

While Hume was an adherent to the classical quantity theory of money, he did recognise the possibility of an increase in the money supply stimulating output if the economy is operating at less than full employment. This is a more Mercantilist or even 'Keynesian' view. Likewise, while in general Hume followed the classical quantity theory in viewing changes in the money supply as affecting prices rather than interest rates, the idea that a higher money supply may result in lower interest rates is also found in Hume's work.

Price-specie flow:
This mechanism demonstrates that an economy aiming for a favourable balance of trade is self-defeating as a natural balance of trade will automatically establish itself. Hume used an analogy to describe it: 'International trade is akin to water in two interconnected vessels constantly seeking a common level'.

William Petty

Petty's use of the concept of surplus inaugurated the beginning of Classical Political Economy, which dominated the discipline until the 1870s. Even after Neoclassical or Marginalist economics replaced the older Classical authors, their method of inquiry was largely retained. That method, along with numerous concepts central to Classical Political Economy, began with the works of Sir William Petty.

Born: 1623, Romsey, Hampshire, England
Importance: Developed concept of surplus which became the mainstay of classical theorists
Died: 1687, London, England

William Petty was a member of the Invisible College, a group of scientists and philosophers that included Thomas Hobbes and Rene Descartes, and which promoted the scientific methods of induction and deduction. While Petty's contributions are often hailed as the origin of the empirical or statistical approach to economics, he was engaged in more than the inductive method – his empirical work was informed by his earlier theoretical framework, especially in *A Treatise of Taxes and Contributions*. Petty was seeking to uncover the laws of operation that gave economic activities regularity or persistence – to discover the economic causes beneath the surface appearances of number, weight and measure.

As capitalism developed, and the ideas of the Mercantilists declined in relevance, the focus of economic reasoning switched from the sphere of exchange to the sphere of production. Nature and labour rather than precious metals were recognised as the source of the nation's wealth. Key here was the concept of an economic *surplus*, or the excess of output over input used in production, including food and other goods required for the subsistence of a labour force. Foreign trade was important as long as it stimulated the development of agriculture and industry, but it

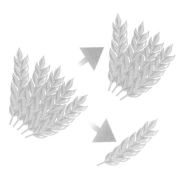

Left: Economic surplus. After setting aside what is needed for survival, surplus is taken by the landlord as rent.

was not the source of wealth and value. All these ideas are found in Petty's best known work, *Political Arithmetic* (1690).

Petty saw production as a circular, surplus-yielding process, and believed that surplus was the key to economic prosperity. He defined surplus as the quantity of corn left after what was set aside for society's reproduction and the replacement of input. The surplus would be extracted by a landlord in the form of rent. It was characteristic of the early Classical political economists to see surplus as rent, rather than profit. Later, surplus would be associated less with agriculture and more with industrial profit. This mirrored the changing relative importance of manufacturing and agriculture in the economy.

Petty distinguished between the 'natural' price and the 'market' price of goods. The natural price of an item was determined by the amount of 'socially necessary' labour time required for its production. The market price could deviate from the natural price when there were transitory influences, such as changes in weather conditions. If the natural price of corn was determined by labour time embodied in it, then the rent or surplus would correspond to the surplus labour applied to its production. Importantly, Petty viewed wages as socially and historically determined subsistence, just as did the later Classical authors.

Richard Cantillon

The reaction against mercantilism and the development of the Classical alternative continued with Richard Cantillon, a banker of French origin. Like Petty, Cantillon emphasised production over exchange, made the distinction between 'intrinsic' value and market price, and viewed wages as determined by socially determined subsistence, all hallmarks of the Classical approach.

Born: 1680, County Kerry, Ireland
Importance: Developed theories on agricultural economics that anticipated the Physiocrats
Died: 1734, London, England

Cantillon's contributions to economic thought come from his manuscript *An Essay Concerning the Nature of Commerce in General*, his only work to remain intact after a fire and murder-robbery in Cantillon's house destroyed the rest of his papers.

Cantillon made important theoretical contributions to economics in the area of production, distribution and value, as well as in money, interest and trade. Land, labour and rural production were the central focus of Cantillon's work. Within this sphere, he distinguished between three social classes: the landowner, the farmer and the labourer. The landowner could manage the land directly or rent it to the farmer. Any farming surplus was appropriated by the landowners. If the land was managed by farmers, the latter would obtain both subsistence and an extra 'profit'. The level of subsistence was determined socially, not as a biological minimum.

The use of land for the production of a surplus depended on the demand of the landlords, nobility and the Prince. Their preferences determined the amount and distribution of the surplus labour. Production of luxuries for the nobility was beneficial in the sense that it extended the cultivation of land and brought more labour into employment. This also meant more land brought into cultivation to provide for subsistence. The increased output of the means of subsistence would allow increased population growth, and thus a growing labour force.

Note that the notion of surplus was not present in the sphere of non-agricultural production. Capitalism finds its origins in agriculture. Especially in France, as opposed to England, during Cantillon's life, many independent artisans still used their own labour and means of production, and appropriated the full value of their product (no surplus was extracted from them). Cantillon's focus on the agricultural sector and land as the fundamental factor of production makes him an important forerunner of the Physiocrats.

Capitalism: An economic system based on the private ownership of the means of production, which sees individuals and companies, motivated by profit, compete with each other in order to sell products in a free market.

In the sphere of monetary exchange, Cantillon showed how an increase in the supply of money could affect the level of prices in the economy. He demonstrated that an increase in the money supply would not affect all industries at the same time and by the same degree, but would be transmitted through a range of industries over time by a chain reaction, at the same time altering the structure of profits, and the real wage. This so-called Cantillon effect would later be re-introduced by Keynes in the *General Theory*.

Cantillon was among the first to reconsider the notion that an increase in the money supply could cause a decline in the level of interest rates. Cantillon dismissed the unique relationship between the supply of money and the level of interest rates. The effect of an increase in the money supply on interest rates would depend on the social class in whose hands the supply of money was appropriated and in what manner it would be spent or invested.

Classical Economics

François Quesnay

The economy is a system, not unlike the human body and its circulatory system, with the flows of goods and money around the various sectors akin to the circulation of blood through the veins and arteries of the human body. This perspective, which seems to arise again and again in the history of economics in one form or another, could be found in Petty, but its real origins are with François Quesnay and the first school of economics, the Physiocrats.

Born: 1694, Merey, France
Importance: Main proponent of the Physiocratic system
Died: 1774, Paris, France

The work of Quesnay and the Physiocrats represents a coherent approach to economic analysis that places the central emphasis on nature and natural laws in explaining economic activity. The Physiocrats divided the economy into different sectors based on types of economic activity. Agricultural, manufacturing and proprietary sectors were linked but not identical to the various social classes of society. Different sectors depended on one another to meet the needs of the economy. The first task was to discover the conditions responsible for the viability or reproducibility of the system: what conditions must be met in order for economic society to be sustained? The next step was to discover the factors accounting for the increase in the national wealth, or total output.

Quesnay's *Tableau Economique* (1759) was an early version of an input-output model. The famous zig-zag design of the Tableau represents the flow of funds between what Quesnay considers the only productive sector, farmers, and what he labels the sterile sector, artisans, starting from the annual total. The landlord in the middle initiates the to and fro of expenditures between farmers and workers by collecting rent from the farmer and spending it on manufactured goods. Manufacturing, the

Physiocrats argued, took up as much value as inputs into production as it created in output, and consequently created no net product. Physiocrats viewed the production of goods and services as consumption of the agricultural surplus; economists now know these to be productive activities which add to economic growth.

Physiocrats saw agriculture as the only productive sector, where the value of agricultural outputs was greater than the value of agricultural inputs (and thus was the surplus-producing sector). The only way to increase productivity of agricultural land was to increase the quantity and quality of tools and implements, *or capital*, applied to it.

The Physiocrats were the first to analyse the economic process as periodic, as opposed to an approach depicting production and consumption occurring simultaneously and concurrently. This is related to the Physiocratic notion of advanced inputs. In order to satisfy the conditions for viability or reproducibility, the same commodities that are used up as inputs must also appear in the output, otherwise production will come to a halt or decrease.

The policy proposals of the Physiocrats were based around the ideas of promoting agriculture, by modernising the sector and increasing its output, sales and income. The increase of agricultural surplus would have feedback effects throughout the economy. One of Smith's advances was to not only see the manufacturing sector as capable of producing a surplus, but as the engine of the developing capitalist economy.

The Physiocrats: considered the first school of economics. Originating in eighteenth century France, they maintained that a nation's wealth was dependent on production rather than accumulation of gold, the mercantilist view, and that the productive yield came solely from agriculture rather than manufactured goods.

Adam Smith

The renowned Scottish political economist and moral philosopher of the eighteenth century, Adam Smith, lived and worked in the era of the first industrial revolution, the expansion of commerce and the monetary economy, the development of science and the ideas of English enlightenment philosophy. All these advancements brought with them a belief in the powers of humanity, freedom and self-determination, together with optimism concerning the future of humankind.

Born: 1723, Kirkcaldy, Fife, Scotland
Importance: Revered as the founding father of economic theory and policy
Died: 1790, Edinburgh, Scotland

Smith was an everyday observer of these movements and they were reflected in his famous work, *An Inquiry into the Nature and Causes of the Wealth of Nations* (1776). In this work, Smith observed the famous diamond–water paradox of use and value:

Nothing is more useful than water; but it will purchase scarce anything; scarce anything can be had in exchange for it. A diamond, on the contrary, has scarce any value in use; but a very great quantity of other goods may frequently be had in exchange for it.

The reason for this has to do with supply and demand, but Smith was unable to explain the paradox economically and it remained unsolved until the development of the neoclasscial marginal–utility theory.

The book was an enormous success and became one of the greatest works of Western civilisation, and the ideas expressed by Smith had a long and lasting effect upon economic theory and policy. Smith is often hailed as the 'father of economics'.

However, it would not be quite fair to wholly attribute to Smith the belief that self-interest is the sole driving force of individual behaviour. On the contrary, human beings are capable of feeling empathy toward their fellow beings. Therefore, the Smithian concept of self-interest in the market exchange should not be associated with a belief in utterly selfish human nature. What is true of human behaviour in market exchange may not hold in other social settings.

With his belief in the natural order bestowed by the invisible hand, Smith opposed arbitrary government intervention into the competitive market economy. *The Wealth of Nations*, in its support for unfettered market activity, became the paradigm for the study of the free market system.

In contrast to his Mercantilist predecessors, Smith saw the wealth of nations not in terms of gold and silver but in a nation's labour and its produce. Production of wealth could be greatly assisted by the division and specialisation of labour. Smith promoted the benefits of national and international division of labour, with an accompanying call for the freedom of international trade. The greater the spread of the market, the more possibilities there are for more specialisation and higher productivity.

Like all the Classical economists, though, Smith foresaw the possibility of capitalism heading toward a stationary or declining state rather than a continuous state of accumulation and advancement. Market saturation, population growth, declining natural resources and falling wage and profit rates were some of the factors cited by Smith that would limit economic growth in market societies.

The Invisible Hand: A force that leads the pursuit of individual self-interest in such a way that it contributes to the common good. Each individual pursuing his or her self-interest contributes to the greatest social well-being. Self-interest and social order are thus reconciled. The quest for individual self-interest becomes the fundamental motive in political economy.

Money and Finance

Although money appeared before the full development of capitalism, it has historically been associated with market economies. In a generalised exchange economy, the extension of the division of labour – or specialisation – is limited by barter-like relations, whereas money allows the extension of the division of labour and exchange. Therefore, money, exchange and the division of labour develop together.

Except in the case of self-sufficient homesteading, where the family or extended family produce everything or almost everything they require and do not participate in trade, producers specialise in the production of a particular good or goods and sell them in exchange for money, then use the money to purchase the other goods and services they require.

Money is often defined by its functions ('money is what money does'). Money functions as a unit of account, a medium of exchange and a store of value. The unit of account (or standard of value) function refers to money being used to measure the comparable worth of different commodities. The medium of exchange function has two aspects: money is used as both a means of purchase, in that it can be exchanged directly for goods and services, and as a means of payment, in that it can be used to settle debts. Finally, the store of value function means that money may also be an end in itself, as a means of accumulating wealth. As a result, money may be saved – and therefore *not spent* – and goods may remain unsold, which can result in a crisis.

Money serves as capital for financing consumption and investment, and thus in part determines the level of economic activity in an area. The level of development of the financial and credit system is therefore of great importance. The availability and terms of credit are central to the operation of modern economies. Modern money systems are 'fiat', or state money systems, where money is not fixed in its exchange rate to gold or any other commodity standard. There are, however, other types of modern fixed exchange rate systems, such as currency unions, currency boards and pegged currencies (one currency fixed to another currency). The issue of fixed versus flexible exchange rates has substantial implications for economic policy.

Theories of money may be divided into two broad categories: metallist and chartalist. Metallist theories view money as arising out of the rational, maximising behaviour of individuals in a market setting. Chartalists view money as a 'creature of the state' (or other central political authority). There are several versions of each of these approaches, with some chartalists taking the position that even a gold or other commodity standard is chartalist, in the sense that the state organises the system, defines the measures and so on.

For many economists, the key issue is acceptability. For money to be valuable, it must be accepted, and its acceptability is often guaranteed by its acceptance at public pay offices, in payment of taxes, for example.

Thomas Malthus

Thomas Malthus is best known for the theory of population growth and its effect on socio-economic welfare and for being the first to emphasise that overproduction and an insufficient level of aggregate demand present problems in an economy. Malthus addressed these theories and other issues in his *An Essay on the Principle of Population, as It Affects the Future Improvement of Society* (1798) and in the *Principles of Political Economy: Considered with a View to Their Practical Applications* (1820).

Born: 1766, Surrey, England
Importance: Socio-economist best known for his theory on poverty and population growth
Died: 1843, Hertford, England

Malthus observed that due to rapid population growth, agricultural activity was expanding onto land of less and less fertile quality. He argued that whereas population was growing geometrically (i.e. exponentially), the means of subsistence were growing arithmetically. This meant that after a certain point there would be insufficient food to meet the needs of a growing population, resulting in starvation and poverty as supply failed to match population growth, creating an upward pressure on prices. Policies to eliminate poverty by means of government subsidies or private charity would only make things worse since, according to Malthus, an increase in well-being of the poorest strata of society would stimulate population growth, further exacerbating the problems of provisioning. Malthus believed that unless population growth could be controlled, poverty was never eradicable. This outlook was one of the reasons economics was labelled the 'dismal science'.

Malthus looked at diminishing returns to land, and rising food prices prompted by population growth; and he noticed that landlords benefitted from expansion as they appropriated more rent. However, whereas workers spent all their wages on subsistence, and capitalists would forego consumption to invest their profits, the landlords were the only class creating demand for products

'Hard as it may appear in individual cases, dependent poverty ought to be held disgraceful.'

Thomas Malthus

and services yet not producing goods and services themselves. Therefore, even though landlords were unproductive, they were crucial to the effective functioning of an economic system because they created demand, which kept prices up, raised profits and preserved the possibility of accumulation. The same was true of other 'unproductive' groups such as servants, statesmen and soldiers. Even though they were not producers, they were important as consumers and that contribution would prevent profits from falling and an economy from stagnating.

No wonder that Malthus spoke in favour of landlords receiving high rents. Higher rents would enable landlords to contribute to the expansion of manufacturing and to make permanent improvements to the productivity of their lands. Malthus' arguments, though often incomplete or difficult to support, were important in the history of economics because of his personal and professional relation with David Ricardo. The Ricardo–Malthus debates were always theoretically significant and had practical policy implications.

David Ricardo

The years between 1776, when Adam Smith's *Wealth of Nations* was published, and 1817, which saw the first edition of David Ricardo's *Of the Principles of Political Economy and Taxation*, were characterised by the rise of a capitalist class as a social and economic elite. Ricardo was writing in the context of an emerging conflict between the interests of landlords and capitalists. While Ricardo's analysis was conducted at an unprecedented level of abstraction, his work was motivated by practical interests in the policy debates of the day, including the British Corn Laws, the Poor Laws and Parliamentary reform.

Born: 1772, London, England
Importance: Major contributions to theories on free trade and rents
Died: 1823, Gloucestershire, England

In 1815, Ricardo published a pamphlet in which he criticised the British Corn Laws, and argued that the elevated rents resulting from restrictions on corn (that is, grain) imports were cutting into profits, slowing investment and growth. Distribution of the national product between landlords, capitalists and workers was of interest to Ricardo, but his prime interest was on the effect of this distribution on future accumulation.

Ricardo believed that the interests of capitalists were the same as the interests of society in general, since capitalist investment was the motor of economic growth. Landlords, on the other hand, were unproductive consumers of luxuries, but they would also benefit from economic growth. Workers, of course, would also benefit from growth. Ricardo's theoretical adversary (but personal friend) was Malthus, who represented the landlord class and viewed its interests as the same as those of society in general.

Malthus saw the General Depression of 1819 in Britain as the result of insufficient effective demand. Since workers spend on subsistence, and capitalists invest most of their profits, in Malthus' view the unproductive consumption of landlords is crucial to boost demand and keep prices up, to raise profits and preserve the possibility of accumulation. Malthus was thus for the restrictions on the importation of cheap foreign grain. Ricardo was against the Corn Laws, as lower prices for necessary consumption would increase profits.

For Ricardo, a rise in the real wage would have no effect on the value of a commodity, as long as there was no change in the amount of labour time embodied in its production. A rise in real wages would have a negative effect on the level of profits since profit was the remainder of production after wages had been paid out. The inverse relation between wages and profits painted a less harmonious portrait of capitalism, highlighting also the conflict between capitalists and workers.

In the Ricardian system, profits are determined on the least productive land – the land that pays no rent. The only way to increase profits on the marginal land, provided there is no increase in the value of the commodity, is to cut wages. The major factor cutting into profits on the non-marginal land is rent.

Ricardo saw falling profits as a result of the extension of cultivation onto less fertile land. The falling rate of profit would eventually lead to a stationary state where profits would be so low that capitalists would have no further incentive to invest. Allowing the cheaper foreign grain into Britain could help stave off the day of reckoning.

John Stuart Mill

John Stuart Mill pioneered the introduction of the human-element approach to economics. Mill was concerned about the unequal distribution of wealth between the classes and whereas earlier political economists had seen this as inevitable, Mill believed the powerlessness of workers should end and social justice be restored.

Born: 1806, London, England
Importance: Proponent of dynamic socio-economics and author of first economics textbook
Died: 1873, Avignon, France

English political economist and humanitarian philosopher John Stuart Mill was educated by his father, James. The elder Mill was also a political economist and educated his son to become a follower of his own ideas. John became fully committed to the advancement of knowledge and improvement of society. However, in many ways he deviated from that extreme individualism and later in life John became more inclined toward benign forms of socialism.

Mill was the author of the very first textbook in economics. His *Principles of Political Economy with Some of their Applications to Social Philosophy* (1848) was a restatement of Classical writers, such as Ricardo and Malthus. The book enjoyed an enormous success and remained the leading textbook until the end of the nineteenth century.

Mill saw society as dynamic and undergoing progressive changes. Old principles had to be restated with a view to new socio-economic conditions. Principles had to be associated with their practical applications and considerations larger than political economy had to be taken into account.

As his predecessors in Classical political economy had done before, Mill saw a tendency toward a falling rate of profit that would lead to a stationary state. Whereas the earlier writers

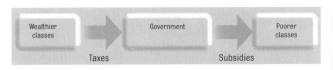

Above: Mill believed that governments should intervene to redistribute wealth from the richer layers of society to the poorer.

associated the stationary state with gloom and poverty, Mill saw it as the blissful final result of economic progress. Society would have achieved a sufficiently high level of wealth; workers would be educated to realise the negative effects of population growth; with a static population there would be no tendency for wages to fall and no reason for further growth in production. High wages and the fall in production would put capitalists in a disadvantaged position and as a class they would disappear. Instead of longing for accumulation, people would address the questions of social justice and an equal distribution of wealth in society. Public spirit would reign rather than individual self-interest.

One of the most important contributions made by Mill was his distinction between the character of the laws of production and those of distribution. Whereas the laws of production are akin to physical laws, the laws of distribution are not found in nature. Distribution is governed by the laws and customs of society; an historical product of human institutions. The nature of distribution varies from society to society and is subject to historical change. Highly concerned with the well-being of workers, Mill saw society's ability to affect distribution as the key to improving the social welfare of the poor and disadvantaged. In order to make the distribution of wealth more equal, society could and should expropriate, redistribute, tax, subsidise and restrict the right of inheritance. Therefore, even private property is not an obstacle to make the distribution of wealth fair.

Karl Marx

While Karl Marx is widely known as a great philosopher, political theorist, activist and historian, it is not so widely known that he was also an economist. His name is more generally and reverentially associated with socialism, and yet Marx wrote very little on that subject compared to his voluminous studies of capitalism.

Born: 1818, Trier, Germany
Importance: Author of *Das Kapital* (1867) and co-founder, with Engels, of Marxism.
Died: 1883, London, England

In his major work, *Capital (Das Kapital)* (1867), subtitled *A Critique of Political Economy*, Marx adopted many of the concepts and theories of the Classical authors and made them his own. The labour theory of value, falling rate of profit, division of labour and many other ideas now associated with Marx can all be found in the works of Adam Smith, Ricardo and their predecessors, such as the Physiocrats and Petty. In fact, it was Marx who introduced the term 'classical political economy' and it was he who defined the characteristics that distinguished classical authors from 'vulgar economists'.

Marx's approach was rigorously historical. He criticised those who 'read' markets back into pre-capitalist modes of production and failed to distinguish the specificity of capitalism as an historical system. For Marx, it is necessary to analyse the social relations of production to understand the 'laws of motion' of capitalism. Conceptual categories such as the 'commodity' and 'capital' cannot be understood in isolation or independently of social relationships.

Marx believed capitalism was a crisis-ridden system, yet viewed it as progressive in the sense that it promoted technological innovation and economic growth, which were just conditions required to create a standard of living that would allow a transition by society to socialism. The heart of capitalism for Marx was the circuit of money capital, depicted by him as M-C-M', where M is money capital, C is commodities and M' > M (M' = M + ?M, and ?M is monetary profits, or the 'surplus value' generated by capitalist exploitation of labour).

Marx believed that the heart of capitalism was capital accumulation, which was generated by the exploitation of labour. He considered exploitation to be an economic concept, the process of surplus value creation resulting from the fact that the value of labour is less than the value created by labour in the sphere of production. Marx called labour 'power variable capital' because its value is self-expanding, while capital goods are constant capital, incapable of varying. Production prices (or natural prices) are regulated by the amount of labour required for production.

> 'Capital is dead labour, which, vampire-like, lives only by sucking living labour, and lives the more, the more labour it sucks.'
>
> *Capital*

Marx's 'laws of motion' include 'dominant tendencies' that might be moderated by government intervention, although the State is not capable of overturning such laws. Therefore, there are strict limits to the impact of economic policy under capitalism and the limits of capital accumulation are internal to the system itself. This is often reflected in the idea that capitalism contains the seeds of its own destruction. However, this need not suggest that Marx held the position that the end of capitalism and the onset of socialism would be automatic; rather political activity, particularly on the part of the working class, was necessary to achieve these ends.

Competition

Although the market economy is decentralised and at times appears chaotic, there is nevertheless some logic to its operation. Competition is one of the factors that gives the economy its 'orderly-like' character.

Competition means rivalrous behaviour, and the touchstone of a competitive economy is that capital is always seeking the highest rate of return. Through capital leaving lower profit rate sectors and moving into higher profit rate sectors, a tendency is established toward a uniform rate of profit within and between industries. When capital departs industries with a lower rate of profit, supply in that market falls and prices will rise, increasing the rate of profit in that market. When capital enters higher profit rate industries, supply increases in that market and prices will fall, causing the rate of profit to fall in that market. This process occurs until profit rates between industries are equalised. A similar process can be seen to take place in the labour market, with workers seeking the highest wage endowing the market with a tendency for wages to be equalised for similar types of employment. Adam Smith described these competitive processes clearly in the *Wealth of Nations*.

Two important components of competition are the market structure of a particular industry, and the competitive behaviour of firms. In terms of market structure, the sise and number of firms in a market will determine the type of competition in that industry. If the firms are relatively small and there are many firms in the market, firms will be 'price-takers', and there will be fierce competition for sales. If the firms are large and there are very few of them in the market, the industry will usually be less competitive and more oligopolistic, with firms that have pricing power. Monopoly is the case where the industry consists of one large firm that has market power and can realise monopoly profits. Even where there are monopolistic or oligopolistic markets, there is still competition. This is because even where there are barriers to entry on the industrial side, finance capital is still mobile, and can exit and enter even monopolistic markets. Monopolistic firms still have to compete for the share of the aggregate market.

Competition *between* buyers and sellers occurs because buyers and sellers have conflicting interests. One side wants the price up, the other side wants the price down, and a competitive bargaining process must occur to determine an agreement. At the same time, there is also competition *among* buyers and among sellers. Sellers compete with other sellers to gain market share and profit, and buyers may try to outbid one another for goods that they want to purchase. Competition forces buyers and sellers to do just the opposite of what they seem to want – it forces sellers to cut price and it forces buyers to bid up the price. This dual struggle – between and among buyers and sellers – is the competitive market mechanism that pushes and pulls the market back to a rough balance of supply and demand.

Government regulation can affect market competition in two main areas. On the one hand, antitrust regulations are intended to break up monopolies (except natural ones that are government sanctioned), and promote competitive markets. There are strict laws against collusion among oligopolistic firms who may be keeping prices artificially high or keeping goods artificially scarce. On the other hand, government regulation also attempts to guard against any excesses of competition, such as bribery, industrial sabotage, spying and deception.

Piero Sraffa

Piero Sraffa was a self-imposed exile from his native Italy as a result of Benito Mussolini's order that he retract statements he made on the Italian banking system. Keynes, who recognised his genius and was desperate to encourage the brilliant young scholar to lecture in Cambridge, brought Sraffa to England.

Born: 1898, Turin, Italy
Importance: Founder of Neo-Ricardian school of economics reviving classical economic principles
Died: 1983, Cambridge, England

Sraffa lectured in Cambridge for a while, but intensely disliked lecturing or speaking publicly in front of large groups, preferring debate and discussion in the small-group format. He was ready to renounce his lectureship, but Keynes, desperate to keep the brilliant young scholar at Cambridge, arranged a number of activities for him: Assistant Director of Research, under which he ran a small seminar for research scholars; Librarian of the Marshall Library; and editor of *The Works and Correspondence of David Ricardo*. Sraffa published relatively few works: a handful of articles, really one major article in English – 'The laws of returns under competitive conditions' (1926) – and one slim book of fewer than one hundred pages, published in 1960: *Production of Commodities by Means of Commodities*. Nevertheless, Sraffa's writings made a significant contribution to twentieth-century economics, both in the critique of Neoclassical economics and the revival of classical political economy.

In his critique of Marshall in the 1920s, Sraffa argued that the standard U-shaped average cost curve, which determined the equilibrium size of the perfectly competitive firm, could not hold up to analytical scrutiny. The descending portion of the curve indicating declining costs was due to increasing returns, while the ascending portion, representing rising costs, was the result of diminishing returns. Sraffa demonstrated that the cases of non-proportional returns that were consistent with both perfect competition and partial equilibrium were empirically insignificant. The upshot was that either perfect competition or partial equilibrium had to be abandoned. In the first case, models of imperfect competition could be explored, while the latter would mean a move to a general equilibrium framework. Sraffa did not believe that the tools for modelling general equilibrium were well-developed enough in the 1920s, and his critique was a major factor in the monopolistic (or imperfect) competition 'revolution' of the early 1930s.

Sraffa's editing of Ricardo's *Works*, which spanned four decades, has been called one of the greatest editorial achievements not only in economics, but in all the social sciences. It was interrupted by a number of new discoveries of manuscripts and a World War, but it was also Sraffa's own painstaking care with which he handled the endeavour that spread the project out over a forty-year period. In addition to the works themselves, Sraffa's general introduction contained some analytical insights that led to new interpretations of Ricardo's approach and also inspired the critique of the Neoclassical theory of capital.

Production of Commodities by Means of Commodities was published in 1960, but the work on it had begun much earlier, in the late 1920s. In fewer than one hundred pages, the book purported to solve the classical problem of value, while providing a critique of both the Marginalist theory of distribution and Marx's labour theory of value. In that sense, Sraffa made both important positive and negative contributions. His positive contribution was to revive Classical Political Economy, while the negative one was a devastating critique of marginal productivity theory.

Alfred Marshall

Alfred Marshall was among the four founders of Neoclassical economics, which is the basic framework that dominates economics to this day. Marshall's *Principles of Economics* (1890) was an enormous success on publication and became the seminal work for generations of economists. Even though Marshall was not the first to draw the curves of demand and supply to determine the equilibrium level of price and quantity, he is regarded as the founder of the theory of supply and demand, the idea that prices themselves are determined by supply and demand.

Born: 1842, London, England
Importance: Introduced partial equilibrium analysis and theory of perfect competition
Died: 1924, Cambridge, England

His belief that mathematics provided a useful analytical approach that could shed light on the small parts of the 'great economic movement' rather than presenting its 'endless complexities' demonstrated that he fully grasped the idea of the interrelated, complex and evolving nature of a socio-economic process. However, such a system would be too complex to comprehend and study as a whole. Therefore, for analytical purposes, he introduced the static method of partial equilibrium analysis. This method would examine the behavior of particular firms or industries, making the *ceteris paribus* (i.e. all other things equal) assumption; that is, one firm or industry was examined as functioning in isolation from everything else.

Marshall made the diagrammatical method of exposition central to the depiction of economic reasoning by using mathematical apparatus, even though he mainly reserved mathematics for the footnotes of his book, and famously remarked about 'burning the math' once it had served its purpose.

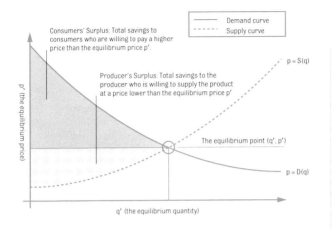

Consumers' Surplus: Total savings to consumers who are willing to pay a higher price than the equilibrium price p'.

Producer's Surplus: Total savings to the producer who is willing to supply the product at a price lower than the equilibrium price p'

Demand curve
Supply curve

$p = S(q)$

The equilibrium point (q', p')

$p = D(q)$

p' (the equilibrium price)

q' (the equilibrium quantity)

Above: The supply and demand curve is a staple of economics. Where the two curves meet is equilibrium, where supply is equal to demand.

A classic example of Marshall's static partial equilibrium analysis was the way he determined an individual firm's market price by the intersection of the countervailing forces of supply and demand. The Marshallian 'scissors', with blades of supply and demand, became a staple of economic analysis.

Marshall developed the theory of perfectly competitive markets and integrated into systematic economic analysis the concepts of: consumer and producer; surplus; diminishing marginal utility; the contemporary distinction between the short period and the long period; the laws of diminishing and increasing returns; internal and external economies; and other concepts that were to become staples of the Neoclassical toolkit. He defined the notion of the 'representative firm', one which is at the average level of development in terms of internal and external economies. The focus of economic analysis was thus shifted to individual agents in their isolation from the rest of the economy and society, a region far removed from the 'grand dynamics' of the Classical economists.

W. Stanley Jevons

Often celebrated along with Marshall, Walras and Menger as one of the four founders of Neoclassical (or Marginalist) economics, W. Stanley Jevons was initially educated in chemistry and mathematics at University College London, but turned to economics after 1857. Jevons's *Theory of Political Economy* was published in 1871 and he was elected a Fellow of the Royal Society in 1872.

Born: 1835, Liverpool, England
Importance: Introduced the marginal utility theory of value
Died: 1882, Hastings, England

While Marshall claimed continuity with the Classics, Jevons argued that marginalism was a clean break with the tradition of Smith and Ricardo. Ricardo had something of a marginal analysis of land and natural resources, but the Classical economists displayed an asymmetric analysis of agriculture and manufacturing – diminishing returns in agriculture, and increasing returns in manufacturing. The Classical conception of diminishing returns recognised both intensive and extensive sources of declining costs, and thus acknowledged both quantitative and qualitative dimensions of the problem. The Neoclassical authors applied diminishing returns to all 'factors of production' (land, labour and capital), an analysis that recognised only the quantitative dimension.

Jevons claimed that value was entirely determined by utility. For Classics such as Smith and Ricardo, utility referred to the usefulness of a particular commodity, but for Jevons and the Neoclassical authors utility was seen as a subjective satisfaction experienced by the consumer rather than an objective characteristic of the good. This emphasis was directly related to the new, greater emphasis on the importance of demand in price theory. For the Classical authors, demand played a very peripheral role, with prices determined by factors such as labour values and other cost-side considerations.

Another key shift in emphasis demonstrated in Jevons' work is the switch from a focus on production to a focus on exchange. This development was related to a move from 'political economy' to 'economics'. For the Classical authors, political economy was concerned with the manner in which societies organised themselves to provide for their material needs. Jevons and other Neoclassical authors rejected this view in favor of one that saw economics as the science of allocating scarce resources among competing uses. This also signalled a new emphasis on scarcity and relative scarcity (relative to unlimited human wants). Jevons himself explicitly favoured a change in the name of the discipline from *political economy* to *economics*, ridding economics of sociological and political aspects and leading to the creation of new disciplines to deal with those subjects.

Jevons was also known for his work on coal and agriculture. In *The Coal Question* (1865), Jevons addressed the concerns expressed publicly at the time that Britain's industrial progress could be impeded by the depletion of coal reserves. Jevons' approach to the question was a Ricardian one: economic growth leading to population increase and an increase in the demand for coal would require extension of excavation to ever deeper and more difficult-to-access mines, raising costs. It is generally maintained that Jevons' scepticism about the coal question was due to his underestimation of the possibility for substitutes, such as oil and gas.

Marginalism: The use of marginal concepts in economics is a defining principle of Neoclassical theorists. These concepts include marginal cost, marginal productivity and marginal utility. Marginalism looks at the effects of small changes occurring in the economic system and how they impact on personal choice and public policy.

Lèon Walras

The French economist Lèon Walras pursued an education and career in both literature and engineering before devoting himself to economics. Walras was made a tenured professor of economics at the University of Lausanne in Switzerland in 1871, where he remained for his career. Walras was the first to apply mathematical analysis to the study of general economic equilibrium.

Born: 1834, Evreux, France
Importance: First economist to apply mathematical method to study of general equilibrium
Died: 1910, Clarens, near Montreux, Switzerland

Economic theory has long been associated with the notion of equilibrium, a concept borrowed from Newtonian physics. The consumer market is in equilibrium when supply of goods in the market equals demand for them. Equilibrium can exist in a particular market, as well as in all markets at the same time. The latter situation is referred to as general equilibrium.

Prior to Walras, the idea of equilibrium was applied to individual markets, holding activities in all other markets constant. Such an equilibrium is called *partial* equilibrium. Walras perceived the concept of partial equilibrium as deficient since no market could be viewed in isolation from other markets. A change in demand and supply conditions in one market would upset the demand and supply conditions in another market through feedback effects caused by the initial change.

In his *Elements of Pure Economics* (1874) Walras proposed a solution to the interdependence of a group of markets. The core of his approach is called 'tâtonnement', or *groping*, a trial-and-error process in which a price is announced by an auctioneer, and the buyers and sellers respond to the price with corresponding bids and offers. If there is an excess of supply over demand at the announced price, then the auctioneer would announce a lower price so that fewer goods would be supplied and more would be demanded. If these bids and offers do not match each other again, new prices would be called out, and there would be another round of bids and offers. The process will continue until a solution is arrived at in which supply equals demand. Once equilibrium has been attained, any price change in any market would disturb the previous equilibrium. A new series of adjustments, led by the Walrasian auctioneer, would take place. Therefore, depending on the change in relative prices, consumers and producers alter the quantities of goods consumed and offered until they find themselves in equilibrium. The *general* economic equilibrium is a situation where consumers and producers in all related markets are in simultaneous equilibrium.

The Walrasian system is highly abstract because in real life such 'auctioneers' do not exist on an economy-wide level. Prices are established imperfectly and there is no built-in mechanism that would lead a system into a simultaneous equilibrium of all markets. However, the importance of Walras's contribution is that he saw all markets as interrelated. This understanding is very important because it signifies that a change in demand or supply conditions in one market would affect demand and supply conditions in another.

Equilibrium: A market is said to be in equilibrium if demand and supply conditions in it equal each other. For example, equilibrium in the labour market will occur when the number of workers willing and able to work is exactly equal to the number of workers firms demand to hire.

Carl Menger

The Austrian economist Carl Menger was one of the founders of Neoclassical economics. However, Menger's theoretical approach to economics was so distinctive it was considered a separate school of thought, and known as 'Austrian Economics'.

The 'coping stone' of Austrian Economics is the theory of value and price determination, the foundations of which Menger laid in his *Principles of Economics* (1871).

Born: 1840, Nowy Sacz, Poland (at the time Neu Sandec, Austrian Galicia)
Importance: One of the founders of Neoclassical economics and forerunner of the Austrian school
Died: 1921, Vienna, Austria

The key to Menger's theory of value is in understanding the concept of utility, or the degree of satisfaction yielded by consumption of goods. The use-value of a good is determined by its ability to satisfy humans' requirements and desires. The concrete use-value consumers attach to goods depends on the concrete need the goods satisfy. Since consumers have various needs of differing priority, consumption is allocated in such a way as to address the most important needs first, and the least important afterwards. As needs are satisfied, the value diminishes with each additional unit consumed, and the amount of utility yielded to the consumer declines as well.

Menger's principle was named the 'law of diminishing marginal utility' wherein he reasoned that the price a consumer is willing to pay is determined by the marginal utility that good will yield. Marginal utility declines with an increase in the volume of consumption, causing an inverse relationship between a good's price and the quantity of it consumed.

If the quantity is limited only the most important needs will be addressed, and the satisfaction of the least important wants will be foregone. Menger concluded that value is thus an entirely

subjective category because it is determined individually in a particular situation.

He explained Adam Smith's diamond–water paradox by arguing that it is not the usefulness of water as a whole that affects price but the usefulness of one unit of water – not total utility but marginal utility. If a man dying of thirst is offered diamonds or a bottle of water, he will surely choose the bottle of water. In this instance, his demand (utility) for water is higher than that for diamonds. Having quenched his thirst, his demand (or marginal utility) for water decreases. Thus, if a man has seven bottles of water, the usefulness of any particular bottle is lower to him than if only one bottle was available. However, the marginal utility for diamonds diminishes at a much lower rate because its supply is limited and demand is high. Hence, diamonds carry higher monetary value than water, even though water is more useful.

Menger also incorporated production goods into his analysis, showing how their value was derived indirectly from the values attached to consumption goods. He demonstrated how market prices and values originated from consumer valuation.

Say's Law of Markets

Say's Law, often crudely stated as 'Supply Creates Its Own Demand', is one of the most important and controversial ideas in economics. Originating in the Classical period, Say's Law in its strongest form is at the heart of Neoclassical macroeconomics, and the key issue in the debate between Keynesian and Neoclassical economists.

Say's Law in its classical form was very different from its more commonly used Neoclassical form. In Classical Political Economy, Say's Law is not much more than the idea that production generates enough income to purchase the goods produced by that production process. This idea is not only true by definition, but is comparable to the national income accounting identity, which states that aggregate output and aggregate income are always equal.

This does not say that all production will necessarily be purchased. There is no mechanism in Classical economic theory to ensure that all production will be bought. Instead, many Classical writers believed that savings would be invested. This was partly a result of their class analysis in which the same social class, namely capitalists, were responsible for both saving and investing. However, this is not the same thing as an analytical mechanism that *ensures* that all savings will in fact be invested. Crucially, there is nothing in the Classical version of Say's Law that ensures that production will be at the full employment level, or that there will be no unemployment in the economy.

In its Neoclassical version, Say's Law goes beyond the Classical definition. There is a Neoclassical *theory* concerning how, under certain conditions (usually described as 'perfect competition' in all markets), not only does production generate enough income to purchase all output, but all production will in fact be purchased. Furthermore, in Neoclassical economics the same theory explains why the level of aggregate output will always tend to be at the full employment level. Finally, and most importantly, while the price mechanism is generally the key, the core of the Neoclassical version of Say's Law is the interest rate mechanism, which tends to equate aggregate savings and aggregate investment at the full employment level of output. In the Classical theory, there is no loanable funds market in the same sense, with a unique equilibrium that equates savings and investment at the full employment level.

The Neoclassical version of Say's Law therefore argues that recessions do not occur because of lack of demand or lack of money. The more goods (for which there is a demand) are produced, the more those goods (supply) can stimulate demand for other goods. Therefore, prosperity should be increased by stimulating production rather than consumption.

It was the Neoclassical version of Say's Law that Keynes sought to overturn with his theory of effective demand. Some have argued that the Keynesian theory of effective demand replaces Say's Law with another, Keynes's Law, that states 'Demand Creates Its Own Supply', which some see as equally one-sided, as both supply and demand are important.

Knut Wicksell

Swedish economist Knut Wicksell was an important Neoclassical economist, but one whose influence extends beyond that school. Wicksell made contributions in both microeconomics and macroeconomics, ranging over the theory of the firm, money and interest rates, technological change, capital theory and taxation and public finance.

Born: 1851, Stockholm, Sweden

Importance: Developed new theory of interest rates and inspired Stockholm School of Economics

Died: 1926, Stocksund, Sweden

Entering Uppsala University at the age of seventeen, Wicksell earned his first degree in mathematics in two years, immediately entered the graduate programme, and finished two-thirds of the requirements by 1875, but then did not complete the final requirement for the graduate degree until ten years later. Although already published and lecturing in a variety of fields, Swedish rules at that time required one to obtain a law degree to teach economics, which Wicksell completed in 1899. He then was appointed to a professorship at Lund University, where he remained until retirement in 1916.

Wicksell's theory of the cumulative process begins with the distinction between the natural rate of interest – the real return on capital – and the market rate of interest – the rate charged for bank borrowing. If the natural rate is higher than the market rate, investors can expect returns to exceed borrowing costs and investment rises, bidding up prices. When the natural rate is lower than the market rate, investment and prices fall. Both of these situations were viewed by Wicksell as cumulative processes that would continue in a self-reinforcing manner, as there are no mechanisms to ensure a return to equilibrium. There are a number of important implications of this analysis.

First, there is a direct policy implication in that stability requires the monetary authorities to set the bank rate equal to the natural rate. Second, both processes entail a divergence between savings and investment, but for investment to exceed savings requires that banks be capable of extending credit to finance investment without a prior supply of savings – traditionally not permissible within the conventional economic framework. This line of thought can lead to both an analysis in which Say's Law ('supply creates its own demand') does not hold and a vision of the economic system where the money supply is determined by market forces, in particular the demand for credit-money, rather than directly controlled by the central bank. Third, in addition to questioning Say's Law, Wicksell's analysis also anticipates Keynes in the sense that monetary factors can influence 'real' variables such as output and employment. These and other aspects of Wicksell's theories became characteristics of the Stockholm School of Economics, many of whose members had been Wicksell's students. In terms of the cumulative process, Gunnar Myrdal would apply the idea much more widely to topics in economic sociology, including poverty and underdevelopment, which also influenced Nicholas Kaldor's work on cumulative causation.

Micro- and macroeconomics:
Microeconomics looks at the behaviour of individual households and firms, while macroeconomics focuses on the national or global economy as a whole. The two are related, as the macroeconomy is comprised of the individual units, and the individual units must act in the context of the macroeconomy.

Irving Fisher

Irving Fisher, an American monetarist of the first half of the twentieth century, was both a clarifier and an originator of economic concepts. He emphasised the dichotomy of real *versus* monetary (nominal) variables. The real economy was determined by factors such as population growth and technology, while money often created illusions, for example when people could not distinguish between their nominal income and its real purchasing power.

Born: 1867, New York, USA
Importance: Formalised the quantity theory of money and developed debt-deflation theory
Died: 1947, New York, USA

In 1911, with the publication of *The Purchasing Power of Money*, Fisher formalised the Classical Quantity Theory of money in a famous equation of exchange: $MV = PT$. M represents the stock of money in the economy; V, the velocity of its circulation; P, the price level; and T, the number of transactions in the economy or the level of economic activity.

Implicit is the notion that the velocity of money circulation is more or less constant, and the level of economic activity is relatively stable, in the short run. Therefore, any increase in money supply would translate to an increase in the level of prices. The equation of exchange later became the basis for the theoretical apparatus of monetarism.

In 1933 Fisher published an article 'The Debt-Deflation Theory of Great Depressions', which became an important contribution to the theory of financial instability. It explained the economic mechanism that could lead to a depression such as that experienced by the United States from 1929 to 1933.

In the same manner, as inflation reduces the real value of debt, deflation increases the real debt burden. Debt is denominated in money, so an increase in the real value of money resulting from a

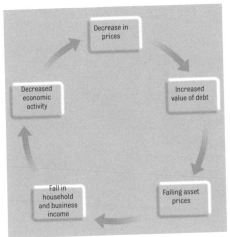

Left: Fisher explained how deflation leads to an increase in the real debt burden.

fall in the price level will increase the real value of household, government and corporate debts. Facing an increase in real debt burden, debtors need to sell their assets in order to meet their obligations. This causes falling asset prices. Also, as firms try to cut costs in order to help pay their debts, they reduce their labour force and buy less from other firms. Thus the incomes of companies across the economy fall, and household incomes too are decreased.

With falling incomes and wide-spread bankruptcy, the aggregate demand in the economy shrinks, causing economic activity to contract and profits to plummet. Decreased demand puts more downward pressure on prices and causes the real value of debt to increase again. The economy enters a vicious cycle of falling prices and increasing debt burdens.

Thus Fisher showed that, paradoxically, the attempt to reduce costs in order to meet debt leads to greater values of real debts. He proposed instead that a boost in the money supply would result in inflation as a cure for the debt-deflation process. Rising prices would cause a contraction in the value of real debt, revert the debt-deflation cycle and provide relief for businesses.

Neoclassical Economics

John Hicks

One of the most influential economists of the twentieth century, John (J. R.) Hicks won the Nobel Prize for his contribution to welfare economics, which analyses market outcomes in terms of their efficiency and the level of social well-being that results.

Born: 1904, Warwick, England
Importance: Introduced the compensation principle, 'traverse' analysis and the IS–LM model
Nobel Prize: 1972
Died: 1989, Gloucestershire, England

Value and Capital (published in 1939) presented a general equilibrium model with aggregate markets for commodities, factors of production, credit and money. Hicks introduced the compensation principle, according to which any economic change would be considered beneficial if, in the new situation, gainers could hypothetically compensate the losers while remaining better off.

Hicks made one of his most important contributions in the field of Neoclassical Keynesian synthesis macroeconomics, which was an attempt to link together Keynes' contributions with the Neoclassical macroeconomic theory. Hicks re-interpreted the ideas expressed by Keynes in *The General Theory* through his famous IS–LM model. Slightly modified, Hicks' model has introduced generations of economists to Keynes. The formal interpretation of Keynes' *The General Theory* by Hicks aimed to show how an economy could be in equilibrium with less than full employment. The downward-sloping IS curve represents an equilibrium in the goods market, whereas the upward-sloping LM curve represents an equilibrium in the money market. The point of intersection of the two curves depicts the general equilibrium in both markets.

The textbook version of the IS–LM model, however, does not involve involuntary unemployment and later in his life, Hicks dismissed the static IS–LM interpretation of *The General Theory*.

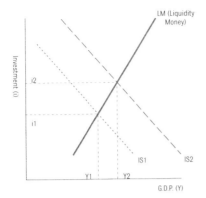

LM (Liquidity Money)

Investment (i)

i2

i1

IS1   IS2

Y1   Y2

G.D.P. (Y)

Left: The IS–LM model shows the relationship between investment and savings, and money liquidity. Here, as investment increases, the IS curve moves to the right (from i1.Y1 to i2.Y2), leading to higher interest rates and economic expansion.

He realised the internal inconsistencies of the model in terms of the different time spans for adjustments in the money market and in the goods market. Hicks even changed the way he signed his articles from 'J. R.' to 'John' Hicks to distance himself from his own earlier positions!

Incorporating the importance of time in economic analysis, Hicks adopted a different approach to depict the dynamics of capitalist development. He became more concerned with the questions of a disequilibrium state, such as the transition of the economy from one growth path to another, structural transformation of the economy and the conditions necessary for continuous reproduction. He called this the 'traverse' analysis in his *Capital and Growth* (1965). He considered the notion of inter-temporal equilibrium and a process of change that consisted of a series of such equilibria. Hicks also made contributions in economic history and monetary analysis.

Paul Samuelson

One of the greatest economic theorists and Nobel-Prize winner, American economist Paul Samuelson was a confirmed believer that mathematics should be integrated into economic analysis. His contributions to economics cover a variety of fields, such as production and consumption theory and welfare economics. Consultations to the United States' government brought Samuelson national and international recognition as an economic advisor. In 1965, he was elected President of the International Economic Association.

Born: 1915, Indiana, USA
Importance: Raised the level of mathematical analysis and made major contributions to a wide number of economic theories
Nobel Prize: 1970

Samuelson's Harvard University PhD thesis was extended into *Foundations of Economic Analysis* (1947), one the most successful textbooks ever written on economics. Another legendary textbook, *Economics: An Introductory Analysis* (1948), has been the best-selling economics textbook throughout the second half of the twentieth century, and has been translated into more than forty languages. For more than fifty years Samuelson's textbooks have shaped and informed generations of economists on the way economics is perceived and on its influence on public policy.

The numerous editions of *Economics* that have followed the initial publication reflect the evolution of Samuelson's thought under the influence of changing economic conditions. The first post-war editions of *Economics* were infused with the fight against post-war unemployment and the role played by government fiscal and monetary policy in promoting income and employment. In later editions, after post-war stabilisation had taken place, his concern shifted from unemployment toward

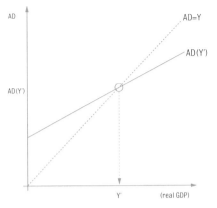

Left: The Keynesian Cross diagram shows the equilibrium point between aggregate demand and real GNP. The line AD=Y is where aggregate supply meets aggregate demand; the line AD(Y'...) shows an increase in demand leading to increased GNP.

inflation. These changes in policy demonstrate that professional views in economics shift in the light of recent experience.

Changes in underlying socio-economic conditions mean that economic theory cannot be static. Samuelson promoted the ideas of John Maynard Keynes by formalising them mathematically and it was through Samuelson's *Economics* that generations of students discovered the 'Keynesian cross' income–expenditure diagram as a device to identify the equilibrium level of national income. This is the level of income at which planned level of spending exactly matches the level of output produced.

In the later editions of *Economics*, following developments in economic theory, Samuelson linked Keynes's ideas with Neoclassical economics into the so-called 'Neoclassical synthesis', an attempt to unify economic theory through its mathematical reformulation.

Samuelson favoured government stabilisation of the economy as a whole, through fiscal or monetary policy, yet advocated the minimum of government intervention to allow for free markets, free competition, and trade.

Milton Friedman

Milton Friedman is one of the most renowned and influential economists of the twentieth century. During a career at the University of Chicago he became the leading figure of the Monetarist school, a staunch defender of free markets and a leading critic of government intervention into an economy. Friedman's contributions have been both scholarly and popular, making his name perhaps the most recognised in the economic discipline.

Born: 1912, New York, USA
Importance: Influential proponent of Monetarist theories
Nobel Prize: 1976
Died: 2006, San Francisco, U.S.A.

Friedman and the Monetarits argued against the efficacy of fiscal and monetary policies to promote full employment and control inflation. Expansionary monetary policy would lead to inflation, whereas expansionary fiscal policy would be entirely offset by reductions in private spending. An increase in government spending, if financed from taxation, would reduce private, disposable income leading to lower levels of consumption, of savings and would cut down investment. If increased government spending was financed from borrowing, the reduction in savings would further reduce private spending, with the net effect of no increase in aggregate expenditure.

He believed that, in the long run, money could not affect the level of real output and that excessive monetary expansion would be inflationary. Freidman perceived inflation as a purely monetary phenomenon that resulted from the excessive supply of money in circulation. Monetarist anti-inflationary policy therefore would require a decrease in the level of money supply or a lowering of the rate of growth of monetary aggregates. Under normal conditions, monetarists recommend an increase in the money supply according to the 'natural' rate of growth of an economy, usually thought to be around three per cent per year, and determined by 'real' factors such as population growth, increase in labour supply and technological improvements.

The theoretical underpinning of Monetarist theory is the Classical equation of exchange: $MV = PQ$. Money supply (M) x velocity of circulation (V) represents the level of aggregate spending, while price level (P) x real output (Q) represents total value of sales.

Since every purchase is also a sale, two sides of the monetary equation are always equal. Friedman held the view that the velocity of circulation (V) is stable and the level of real output (Q) tends to full employment. In this way, there is a direct relation between money supply and prices with the causality running from the former to the latter; as the money supply increases with a constant V, there will be a corresponding increase in Q (with P remaining constant), or an increase in P if there is no increase in the quantity of goods produced.

Friedman's notion of the 'natural rate of unemployment' became an important concept. The 'natural rate' was the minimum rate of unemployment consistent with stable prices. Attempting to reduce unemployment beyond the natural rate would ultimately lead to inflation. Friedman blamed the stagflation that was experienced in the 1970s on expansionary monetary policies that attempted to achieve full employment.

The American's popularity was increased by his presentation of the television series and accompanying book, *Free to Choose*, in 1980. This and his earlier book, *Capitalism and Freedom* (1962), signified that markets allow the maximum of political freedom and economic progress, and offer solutions to most of the problems of a modern capitalist society, while governments are responsible for loss of freedom and economic hardship, and government intervention is rarely appropriate.

Friedrich August von Hayek

The roots of the Austrian School of Economics go back to Carl Menger, but it is Friedrich Hayek who best represents the School in the twentieth century. He is best known for his defence of liberal democracy and free-market capitalism against socialist and collectivist thought in the mid-twentieth century, and his followers, as well as those of his contemporary Ludwig von Mises, make up the contemporary Austrian School of Economics.

Born: 1899, Vienna, Austria
Importance: Leader, with Mises, of the 'Austrian economics' school of thought
Nobel Prize: 1974
Died: 1992, Freiburg, Germany

Hayek studied law and political science at the University of Vienna before working as a research assistant at New York State University. During the early 1930s, he was at the London School of Economics, but eventually moved to the United States, where many of his students went on to elaborate the framework and create institutions that kept the Austrian approach alive. Hayek's gaining of the Nobel Memorial Prize in 1974 led to a revival of the Austrian school, and his ideas are said to have influenced US President Ronald Reagan and British Prime Minister Margaret Thatcher, who both held political office during the 1980s. Austrian departments and institutes have thrived, to this day, in New York, Auburn and George Mason Universities.

Hayek enjoyed a reputation as a leading economic theorist and, along with Ludwig von Mises, made important contributions to the Austrian side of the socialist calculation debate. Some Neoclassical economists argued that their price theory could be applied to a planned economy, and that it might work there better than in a capitalist system. However, Mises and Hayek objected, arguing that it was impossible for a collectivist system to obtain dispersed knowledge that could only result in orderly outcomes within the market framework. The Austrians also had political objections to socialism, stated most famously in Hayek's 1944 book *The Road to Serfdom*.

Hayek and Mises also influenced the Austrian theory of the business cycle, which led to specific implications for issues related to money, banking and central banking. In direct contrast to Keynes, the Austrians viewed recession and depression as the result of bad monetary policy, in particular excess money creation which led to inflation, thus damaging the price-signalling effects that coordinated the balance between the capital and consumption goods industries. This analysis led to proposals for free banking and private money creation. As with most issues, Hayek and Mises put forward the view that the market disciplined economic factors in ways that government intervention did not, meaning that free markets would result in better outcomes. Hayek also held that, with few exceptions, government intervention only made matters worse.

In the later years of his career until his retirement in 1968, Hayek began to focus on political philosophy and psychology, although he did also continue to work on economic issues. As well as his contributions to the field of economics, he is remembered as one of the greatest political philosophers of the twentieth century.

Planned economy: An economic system in which a single agency makes all decisions about the production and allocation of goods and services. It is used most often to refer to a state or government which regulates the factors of production and makes all decisions about their use and the subsequent distribution of income (such as the former Soviet Union, Cuba or Korea).

Robert Mundell

Canadian-born Robert Mundell is an originator of the Optimal Currency Area (OCA) paradigm, the theoretical foundation for currency unions. The currency of the European Union, the Euro, was explicitly based on Mundell's ideas and he is often referred to as the 'father of the Euro'. Mundell received his PhD from the Massachusetts Institute of Technology in 1956 and has been on the faculty of Columbia University since 1974.

Born: 1932, Ontario, Canada
Importance: Theories on OCA and supply-side economics
Nobel Prize: 1999

Mundell's proposition is that, under certain conditions (primarily the free mobility of labour, price and wage flexibility) a common currency will be more efficient for a particular geographic region as it reduces transaction costs associated with multiple currencies. Mundell applied the idea to Europe, arguing that the benefits of a common European currency would be greater than its implementation costs. His optimal characteristics for the merger of currencies or the creation of a new currency are: labour mobility across the region; capital mobility and price and wage flexibility across the region; an automatic fiscal mechanism to redistribute money to areas which have been adversely affected by the first two characteristics. This usually takes the form of taxation redistribution to less developed areas of a region.

There are several objections to the OCA argument. Among them, a number of empirical and historical objections. A most striking fact of economic life is the one government–one currency link. In addition, OCA theory would predict that the break-up of nation-states would not tend to result in each of the new states having its own currency, but that is almost always what is observed, for example in the former Soviet Union and Yugoslavia.

A second objection is that nations sacrifice their monetary sovereignty when joining a currency union.

An analogy is sometimes made between nations in the European Monetary Union (EMU) and states in the USA. The problem with this is that in the USA there is fiscal authority at federal level, so that coordination with monetary policy is possible, and individual states can fall back on assistance from the federation. If the EMU had a fiscal branch this would be different, but instead agreements such as the Maastricht Treaty strictly limit fiscal policy of the member nations.

Optimal Currency Area (OCA): A geographical region in which it would maximize economic efficiency to have the entire region share a single currency.

Mundell's OCA approach contrasts with the Chartalist approach originally associated with Knapp, which views 'money as a creature of the state'. This approach is immune to the two objections to the OCA theory cited above. The one government–one money link is seen as an historical and empirical confirmation of the Chartalist theory, and the same link guarantees the ability to coordinate fiscal and monetary policies. Strictly speaking, it is not only currency union, but also other fixed exchange rate systems that have the problems cited by the Chartalists. These would include systems based on 'pegged' currencies (where the currency of one nation is fixed) to the currency of another, as for example in Argentina prior to 2000, where the peso was fixed to the US dollar and currency boards.

In addition to his work in OCA theory, Mundell's contributions have been in the areas of supply-side economics and tax policy, exchange rates and balance of payments.

Growth Theory

Growth is the increase of real per capita output, or total production of goods and services relative to the size of the population. But economic growth is not purely quantitative; it is also qualitative. Growth does not simply result in a larger version of the same economy, as if blowing up a balloon. Growth is disproportional and disruptive – it transforms structural and technological organisation, with important social as well as economic changes in the institutional character of the system.

The Classical theories of Adam Smith, David Ricardo and Karl Marx were essentially theories of growth, or capital accumulation. They were interested in both the causes and consequences of economic expansion, and the conditions for its continuation. Growth was not guaranteed in the Classical theories – quite the contrary: the term the 'dismal science' was used specifically because most of the Classical authors viewed the likely future of capitalism as one of either a declining or stationary state, rather than a progressive or advancing one.

Growth was not a primary topic of early Neoclassical economics, as they were interested in the distribution of a given output, although later Neoclassical theories of growth were put forward, and continue today, sometimes even knowingly or unknowingly echoing some of the Classical themes. Interest in growth was revived with Schumpeter and Keynes. Keynes put forward the notion that the level of output and employment were determined by the level of aggregate demand. His colleague, Roy Harrod extended this to the idea that the growth of output and employment were determined by the growth of aggregate demand. Schumpeter brought issues of innovation, technical change and entrepreneurship into the analysis of the growth process.

An important distinction in most growth theories is that between exogenous and endogenous growth. Exogenous refers to factors originating outside the economic system, while endogenous refers to market forces of some kind. The classical theories were for the most part endogenous ones, for example where technological change is driven by competition, as in Marx. Neoclassical versions of endogenous growth models emerged in the latter part of the twentieth century, often claiming as 'new' ideas that could be found in Adam Smith.

In recent years, the focus has moved from growth pure and simple to *what kind* of growth, in particular with reference to the impact on the natural environment. The term 'sustainable development' emerged to indicate economic progress that preserves the ecological basis for future economic activity. Thus the rates of use of natural resources and the issues of pollution emissions, as well as global warming and other challenges, were incorporated into research on growth. In addition, research on 'happiness' has shown that growth does not necessarily increase human happiness, raising a number of important questions and concerns. At the same time, while people 'do not live on bread alone', economics cannot ignore the basic preconditions for living a life at all – necessary material provisioning.

In his chapter on the 'stationary state' in his *Principles of Political Economy and Taxation* (1848), John Stuart Mill was one of the first to argue that modern industrial societies might choose to forego additional growth and focus on distribution. Contemporary ecological economists and others follow Mill in their support for a 'zero-growth' or 'steady-state' economy.

John Maynard Keynes

John Maynard Keynes was one of the most important and influential economists of the twentieth century and perhaps of the whole modern era. The son of Cambridge economist John Neville Keynes, and a student of Alfred Marshall, Keynes was brought up on the powerful Neoclassical paradigm, but was always a somewhat wary practitioner of Marshall's framework.

Born: 1883, Cambridge, England
Importance: Introduced modern macroeconomics and the Keynesian revolution in theory and policy.
Died: 1946, East Sussex, England

Eventually, he broke with Marshall and put forward an alternative approach to explain persistent unemployment during the Great Depression, which is widely regarded as launching the modern macroeconomics, as well as the commencement of the Keynesian revolution in theory and policy.

Keynes put forward an alternative view of capitalism as a monetary production economy, and rejected the traditional separation of monetary and 'real' factors. In this latter perspective, money was seen as a 'veil' lying over the real economy of population and labour supply, technology and real stocks of capital and natural resources. In Keynes, money is real, and monetary variables can affect real outcomes. This led Keynes to a unique approach to the savings–investment relation, rejecting the loanable funds model and putting forward alternative theories of the determination of savings and investment. In the loanable funds approach, he determined that savings is a positive function of the rate of interest, and investment is a negative function of the rate of interest, and their unique equilibrium was one of the keys to why Neoclassical economics viewed the economy as self-adjusting to the full employment of land, labour and capital. Keynes viewed savings as a function of income, and investment as determined by a variety of factors, including investor expectations of future economic conditions and business and political climate, with interest rates playing a much weaker and more indirect role in investment determination. Moreover, Keynes viewed investment as the driving force, and savings the passive residual, so the causal relation was opposite that of the Neoclassical framework, where savings determines investment through variations in the interest rate. Finally, Keynes found that savings and investment could be equal at a whole range of levels of output, only one of which was full employment, whereas in the Neoclassical model of full employment, savings equal to investment is the unique macroeconomic equilibrium. Thus Keynes demonstrated the theoretical possibility (and likelihood) of the an economic system operating at an unemployment macro-equilibrium, and the existence of involuntary unemployment due to deficiencies in effective demand. This provided the theoretical justification for interventionist policies to stimulate output and employment, and so was a critique of laissez-faire.

Keynes had considerable influence in international economics and policy and maintained a number of high-level and sometimes sensitive posts in the British government off and on throughout his life. He served as a representative at the Treaty of Versailles peace conference in 1919 which officially ended the First World War and he led the British delegation at the Bretton Woods Conference in 1944; Keynes had considerable influence in international economics and policy. Although many of Keynes' proposals were rejected by the United States, the post-Second World War international monetary system bore his stamp until its breakdown in the early 1970s.

Don Patinkin

Don Patinkin, an American-Israeli economist and President of the Israeli Economic Association in 1976, is known for his numerous contributions to post-war monetary theory, foremost among them his 'Grand Neoclassical Keynesian Synthesis' or simply the Neoclassical synthesis.

Born: 1922, Chicago, USA
Importance: Major contributions to monetary theory, especially the Neoclassical synthesis
Died: 1995, Jerusalem, Israel

The Neoclassical synthesis was perhaps the most ingenious of the several responses by economists to Keynes' *General Theory*. It demonstrated that some of the Keynesian contributions to macroeconomics could be incorporated into the broader Neoclassical framework without affecting the central proposition that if wages, prices and interest rates are flexible, then an economy will tend to full employment in the long run. The Keynesian results of involuntary unemployment and insufficient aggregate demand would be obtained only if price or factor-price rigidity were present in an economy, in the short run.

While at a theoretical level Patinkin's work illustrated that the Keynesian and Neoclassical theories were compatible, when it came to policy Patinkin supported Keynesian fiscal and monetary tools rather than awaiting market self-adjustment. His theory/policy split was characteristic of all the Neoclassical synthesis authors, such as Samuelson, Tobin and Modigliani.

The core of Patinkin's argument became known as the real balance effect, because it relies on the way in which changes in the real value of cash balances can stimulate output and employment. There are two aspects to the argument: the direct real balance effect and the indirect real balance effect. Both begin with the proposition that under conditions of unemployment, firms will slash prices to try to unload excess inventories. Resulting deflation increases the real value of money.

In the direct real balance effect, Patinkin argued that the increase in the value of cash directly stimulates consumption and investment by consumers and investors who feel richer due to the increased value of their holdings, setting off a process that pushes output and employment toward full employment.

In the indirect real balance effect, his argument centred on the increase in the real value of cash balances that indirectly stimulate consumption and investment spending through lowering interest rates. Falling prices decrease the amount of money required for normal transactions to free up cash available for speculative purposes. The increase in the demand for securities (stocks and bonds) bids up bond prices, lowering the cost of borrowing; consumption and investment rise, and output and employment expand toward full employment.

Patinkin's ideas are found in his *Money, Interest and Prices: an Integration of Monetary and Value Theory* (1956). While this approach sought to reconcile Keynes' contributions with the standard approach, it incorporated a number of Keynes' insights into the synthesis. The importance of conducting macroeconomic analysis, a central role for money as a direct, determining variable, the multiplier concept and even Keynes' liquidity preference theory of the rate of interest were all brought into the analysis.

Real balance effect:
The stimulation of output and employment caused by increasing consumption due to a rise in real balance of wealth, particularly during deflation. Also known as the Pigou Effect having first been proposed by the English economist Arthur Pigou in 1943.

Joan Robinson

Joan Robinson belonged to a group of Cambridge economists that surrounded John Maynard Keynes and who helped develop and extend Keynes' *General Theory*. The group set out to explore the true meaning of Keynes' ideas and its members came to be known as the Post-Keynesian economists. They claimed that interpretations, other than theirs, of Keynes' *General Theory* had significant flaws.

Born: 1903, Surrey, England
Importance: Laid foundations for theory of imperfect competition
Died: 1983, Cambridge, England

Robinson made significant contributions to many other fields in economics as well, and was perhaps one of the most eclectic economists. However, she was not interested in formal economic theory for its own sake. On the contrary, political aspects of economic problems and their possible resolutions were her source of inspiration. Robinson's writings were politically coloured, and this distinguished her economics from conventional analysis about which she was very sceptical. For this reason she became one of the most well-known critics of conventional economic theory.

The critical aspects of Robinson's thinking were already evident when she produced *Economics of Imperfect Competition* (1932). Recognising the unrealistic assumptions that conventional theory made about the nature of competition, she laid the groundwork for analysing market structures that were neither truly competitive (i.e., an infinite number of small firms produce diverse products), nor true monopolies (i.e., the exclusive control by one firm of the production of a particular product). Empirical evidence supported the existence of firms of various sizes that produced differentiated products (i.e., goods of the same category that differ slightly from each other in terms of quality and

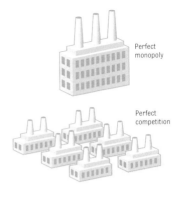

Perfect
monopoly

Perfect
competition

Left: A perfect monopoly calls for just one supplier of a good, while perfect competition calls for an infinite number of suppliers producing homogenous goods; in reality both are rare.

characteristics). Product differentiation was the key to establishing consumer preference for a particular firm/product. Robinson's foundations of the theory of imperfect competition are today found in every microeconomics reference work.

Robinson is also known for launching a large-scale controversy about the measurement of capital. Her arguments made clear the difficulties in measuring diverse units of capital and incorporating them into formal economic analysis. The debate developed into the Cambridge Capital Controversies of the 1960s and 1970s, and produced significant contributions to the theories of capital and growth. It led Robinson to publish her major work *The Accumulation of Capital* (1956).

Robinson insisted that economic analysis should be conducted in a historical context, otherwise economic theories and practical experience become inconsistent. She elaborated Keynes' ideas of fundamental uncertainty, the impact of expectations on investment decisions, and the role of investment and aggregate demand in economic growth. She insisted that unemployment was a normal feature of capitalism, not a temporary maladjustment, and government intervention was therefore necessary to provide for full employment. These ideas became the cornerstones of the Post-Keynesian approach.

Joseph E. Stiglitz

John Maynard Keynes showed that the existence of involuntary unemployment was consistent with the normal workings of the economic system. Joseph E. Stiglitz would start with the equilibrium framework and ask how the results would be modified if one of the assumptions of perfect competition, such as perfect information, was relaxed.

Born: 1943, Indiana USA
Importance: Developed theory of imperfect information
Nobel Prize: 2001

Joseph E. Stiglitz gained a PhD from Massachusetts Institute of Technology (MIT) in 1967 and became a professor at Yale before he was thirty years old. He served as the Chairman of the US Council of Economic Advisers from 1995 to 1997, was Chief Economist of the World Bank, and since 2000 has been University Professor at Columbia University and Chair of Columbia's Committee on Global Thought.

The 'economics of information', for which he was awarded the Nobel Memorial Prize in 2001, is part of his wider contribution to the 'New Keynesian' economics. The analysis of imperfect information was one important example of the implications of market imperfections of numerous kinds. Imperfect competition, market failure and the policies appropriate for the outcomes associated with them are the hallmark of Stiglitz and the New Keynesians.

The New Keynesian approach is firmly rooted in Neoclassical microeconomics, and the only link to Keynesian economics is in the policy conclusions. Keynes did not achieve his results by assuming market imperfections, but rather showed that the existence of invountary unemployment was consistent with the normal workings of the economic system. In contrast, Stiglitz would start with the equilibrium framework and ask how the results would be modified if one of the assumptions of perfect competition, such as perfect information, was relaxed.

Some of the conclusions reached by Stiglitz had something of a Marxian flavour. In a 1984 article with Carl Shapiro, unemployment was viewed as disciplining workers, as in Marx's concept of the reserve army of labour. With full employment, worker bargaining power is stronger as jobs are plentiful and there is no excess labour supply. Workers do not feel compelled as would be the case if there were queues of unemployed waiting to take their positions.

During his tenure at the World Bank, Stiglitz courted controversy with his criticisms of the policy framework of the International Monetary Fund, the World Bank and the US Treasury, known as the Washington Consensus. In particular, Stiglitz criticised the approach to economic development in Asia, Africa and Latin America and to the transitional economies of the former Soviet Union. It entailed a market approach emphasising privatisation, free trade, and structural adjustment programmes, including deregulation and budget balancing.

In his 2002 book *Globalization and its Discontents*, Stiglitz takes on the Washington Consensus, highlighting the dangers of fiscal conservatism, such as high interest rates and low government spending. He consistently pointed out the economic success of nations that went against the recommendations of the IMF and the Consensus, such as China, while those nations that followed their recommendations failed to achieve the promised results.

Uncertainty, Risk and Information

Pre-Keynesian economics tended not to consider the uncertainty that consumers, investors and even policymakers face concerning economic circumstances. The Neoclassical notion of perfect competition includes the assumption that economic actors have perfect knowledge and foresight. It was Keynes, along with Chicago economist Frank Knight, who raised the issue of economic uncertainty and its implications, and made the important distinction between uncertainty and risk.

Any decision about the future may be called a risk if the nature and amount of information available means that a statistical probability of a particular event occurring may be calculated. When such information is not available, a situation may not properly be called a risk; instead, the decision-maker is said to be operating under conditions of true uncertainty. As Keynes famously remarked, 'We simply do not know'.

Even under conditions of risk, the decision to act or not to act depends on how confident the decision-maker is that they will 'beat the odds'. Keynes believed that not much investment would take place based purely on cold calculation. Instead, investors were led by 'animal spirits' – the *will* to act.

Neoclassical economists took up the topic of 'imperfect information' rather than uncertainty. The assumption of perfect information was relaxed, and models of imperfect competition (where the conditions for perfect competition – where no producer or consumer has the market power to influence prices – are not satisfied) were devised to ask how results would be modified. One example of this is 'asymmetric information', where the two parties involved in a transaction have access to different kinds and/or amounts of information. Take the used car market. Here, the owners know more about the quality of the cars than the buyers. Buyers who know that there are good and bad cars will rationally pay a price based on the average quality of the cars. Owners will then see that the better cars are underpriced, and may remove those from the market. As a result, the average quality of the cars available will fall, as will the price buyers are willing to pay. The better cars will again be underpriced, and if they are removed from the market, another round will follow.

Another famous model of imperfect information is the 'prisoners' dilemma', a basic model of game theory. Two people are arrested for burglary and possessing stolen property. The two are put in separate rooms and not allowed to communicate. They are separately told that if they both confess, they will both be sentenced to three years for burglary. If neither confesses, they can only be convicted of the lesser crime of possessing stolen property, and will be sentenced to one year. If only one confesses, that prisoner will be released and the other will get a harsher sentence of five years. In this situation, although the best solution is for neither to confess, both will have the incentive to confess. If the other confesses, confessing would result in the three-year sentence, while not confessing would result in a five-year sentence. If the other does not confess, confessing would result in being let go, while not confessing would result in a one-year sentence. This result is 'suboptimal equilibrium', and can be applied to many economic circumstances.

Abba Lerner

Over fifty years of economic scholarship, Lerner spanned both microeconomics and macroeconomics; Neoclassical and Keynesian frameworks; and theory and policy. He had faith in markets and a commitment to democratic socialism.

Born: 1903, Bessarabia, Russia

Importance: Developed theory of market socialism known as the Third Way.

Died: 1982, Florida, USA

Lerner's most enduring contribution is known as Functional Finance. He viewed the *laissez-faire* position as a refusal to take hold of the 'economic steering wheel', and famously liked to use the analogy of driving an automobile to justify and defend the use of government controls that 'steered' the economic system onto the right path.

Lerner encouraged government to use its fiscal and monetary authority to maintain total effective demand at full employment level, to prevent inflation and keep interest rates at the level required for the optimal amount of investment. He did not consider the principles of 'sound finance' (the view that government budgets should be balanced and big national debts avoided) as a theoretical obstacle to this because government could issue as much money as was required to steer its economy in the right direction. Lerner was therefore clearly in the Keynes-Knapp-Chartalist school. *Money as a Creature of the State* (1947) provided the key to understanding the possibility and effectiveness of Functional Finance.

Lerner's theory, though, has been subject to a number of objections. In particular, it was criticised for promoting big government deficits. However, Functional Finance simply sees the federal budget and the management of the national debt as a *means* to economic prosperity. The size of the budget is not an end *in itself*, but a *means to an end*. Functional Finance judges economic policy decisions by their effect upon the economy, and rejects any doctrine about what is sound or unsound. Lerner did not view taxation and government borrowing as funding operations undertaken by the state because the latter needed money to spend. He saw government borrowing as a means of managing monetary reserves and controlling the level of short-term interest rates, whereas taxation was a means of managing aggregate demand to fight inflation.

Lerner coined the term 'upside-down economy', by which he meant an economy in which traditional economic principles do not hold. He noted that when there is unemployment, inefficiency sets in. An increase in savings (for example) can slow the economy down by reducing spending, and technical efficiency can result in more unemployment.

Lerner was initially concerned with demand-side inflation and saw taxation as a means of controlling it. However, he later became more concerned about supply-side or cost-push inflation. He noticed that inflation did not begin at the full employment level, but well before that point, and he introduced the terms 'low-full employment' and 'high-full employment', anticipating the idea of a non-accelerating inflation rate of unemployment (NAIRU).

In the face of these developments, Lerner dedicated himself to the study of stagflation (simultaneous recession and inflation), and the evaluation and formulation of various income policies, market anti-inflation plans (or MAPs) and wage–price controls.

Nicholas Kaldor

The Hungarian economist Nicholas Kaldor was educated at the London School of Economics, and then Cambridge, to become one of the most distinguished economists of his time. Kaldor's contributions to microeconomics and macroeconomics covered both theoretical and policy issues and were most notable in the areas of monetary theory and welfare economics, as well as the theory of development and growth.

Born: 1908, Budapest, Hungary
Importance: Major contributions to monetary theory and welfare economics
Died: 1986, Cambridgeshire, England

Kaldor was a fierce opponent of monetarism and in his later years rejected the notion of a determinate economic equilibrium in favour of an indeterminate dynamic adjustment rooted in cumulative causation and a path dependency framework. This framework was proposed by Kaldor as an alternative tool for analysing the global capitalist economy.

In *The Scourge of Monetarism* (1982), Kaldor put forward the view that the demand for a money supply be controlled by a central bank and be determined by market forces. The creation of excess reserves by a central bank would not automatically result in increased borrowing. Conversely, a lack of excess reserves would not set limits to the lending capacity of a banking system. Central and private banks could accommodate the demand for credit, credit would be extended and investment would take place, income and savings would be increased and redeposited into the banking system, replenishing the reserves depleted as a result of the initial loans and even expanding reserves.

In economic analysis, Kaldor put emphasis on cumulative causation or historical path dependency of a system as an alternative to the notion of a determinate equilibrium outcome.

An *a priori* determined equilibrium was unlikely since the final outcome depended on a series of preceding adjustment processes within an economy. There could therefore be many potential outcomes that could emerge in the dynamic adjustment process. Any particular outcome would depend on a series of adjustment processes preceding it. Moreover, the dynamics of an economy represented continuous shifts in final outcomes. Hence, there could be no final equilibrium outcome but a series of disequilibrium adjustments. Kaldor thus stressed dynamics and historical continuity versus equilibrium. Kaldor's economics is often referred to as economics without equilibrium.

Kaldor's cumulative causation was about positive feedback, wherein, particularly in the manufacturing sector, increasing returns would lead to productivity growth that would result in competitive success in the global markets, while sluggish demand meant slow productivity growth and competitive failure. Kaldor used this model to explain the 'polarisation thesis' concerning the division of the world into developing industrial economies on the one hand and stagnant underdeveloped economies on the other.

The British economist served as an advisor to the British Labour Party, advised governments and central banks around the world and served with the United Nations. A prolific writer, Kaldor is considered an important figure of the Post-Keynesian approach.

Polarisation thesis:
The theory that the division of the world into rich industrial nations and poor underdeveloped nations is the result of cumulative causation. Industralised countries specialised in manufacturing, and poor nations were assigned the role of producers of primary products, making the latter less competitive.

James Buchanan

James Buchanan is regarded as the father of public choice theory, a theory that changed the way economists viewed the role of government and politicians. Buchanan's proposition was that rational behaviour of self-interested individuals was not confined to the economic sphere, but was observable in the public sector, and that viewing the public sector in such a way offered insights into politics and policies.

Born: 1919, Tennessee, USA
Importance: Renowned for his work on Public Choice Theory
Nobel Prize: 1986

James Buchanan gained his PhD in economics at the University of Chicago in 1948, and began his teaching career at the University of Tennessee. He held positions at a number of universities, including the University of Virginia and George Mason University, where, at the time of writing, he remains active.

At a time when Keynesian economics were highly influential and formed the basis for post-Second World War policy, Buchanan was its critic on a number of basic issues, including methodological ones. For Buchanan, the high level of aggregation of Keynesian macroeconomics was contrary to the methodological individualism appropriate for his conception of a democratic society. Such an aggregate approach also served to hide or diminish the power of basic economic principles operating at the individual level, such as opportunity cost. It led to Buchanan's focus on initiating debate over government budget deficits and the national debt.

His position on government budgeting was consistent with the 'deficit hawk' view of deficit and the debt. Buchanan saw government borrowing to finance deficit as competing with the private sector for a given supply of loanable funds, crowding out private spending and pushing up interest rates. The national debt imposed a burden on future generations, which was viewed as immoral. Buchanan has long advocated a constitutional amendment to balance the budget.

Buchanan was opposed to the increasing formalism of economics, whether formal modelling or high-tech empirical approaches. Instead, he looked back to the origins of economics (or political economy) in moral philosophy. Like Adam Smith, Buchanan emphasised economic exchange and the legal and institutional setting required for satisfying the mutual advantage of economic factors. The focus on institutional and legal conditions led Buchanan to the analysis of rules, rule-setting and rule-following behaviour. This places Buchanan closer to the Classical political economists than to his contemporaries, many of whom conceived of economics as a 'science' – something Buchanan objected to – for him economics can be scientific in the same sense as philosophy, but unlike physics.

Public choice theory: Rejects the idea that politicians and policy makers can be or are motivated to behave to increase the social welfare of society. Their primary motivation is re-election, increasing their political power and exploiting economic opportunities. Thus there is an inherent tendency toward maintaining and increasing the size of government.

Robert Eisner

Robert Eisner is best known for his contributions to fiscal and monetary policy, investment, and his proposals for improvements in the methods of national income accounting.

Born: 1922, Brooklyn, USA
Importance: Major
contributions to fiscal policy
especially national income
accounting
Died: 1998, Illinois, USA

For Eisner, the fundamental importance of the federal deficit was in its effect on private spending. A federal deficit results in a private sector surplus because government spending injects income in the aggregate flow of expenditure, while taxation withdraws income from that flow. A deficit will therefore have a net positive impact, as spending (or injections) is greater than tax revenues (or withdrawals). Reducing the federal deficit therefore reduces private sector expenditure. Eisner saw no logical or empirical support for the claims that deficits cause high interest rates or inflation.

A bigger federal deficit and a growing national debt are useful in stimulating an economy in a recession caused by insufficient spending. However, if an economy is already at full employment, and operating at or near full capacity, a rise in aggregate demand will cause inflation. Eisner argued that the logic of an economy with unemployed resources is different from the economy running at full employment and full capacity. High deficits at full employment will be inflationary, but if there is unemployment and slack in the economy, deficits will stimulate output and income, not prices.

Eisner's contribution to national income accounting methods included a proposal that inflation reduces the real value of debt and thus government accounts should be systematically restated to reflect the results of inflation. As an alternative way to look at

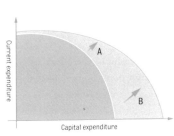

the size of the debt, Eisner proposed to count it as a per cent of gross domestic product (GDP). He made the point that how much debt one can afford depends upon one's wealth and income, so that an economy with a large GDP can afford a large budget deficit and national debt.

Another of Eisner's proposals was that federal government should keep a capital account. Businesses and state and local governments make a distinction between current and capital spending. Spending this year for goods and services that will be used this year (for example, labour) goes onto the current account. Spending this year on goods that will be used several years in the future (for example, land and buildings) goes onto the capital account and the total cost is divided over the lifetime of the investment. Federal government does not keep capital accounts, so all spending goes onto current account. Thus, there appears *this year* to be huge expenditure, but the investment will benefit society for many years into the future. By separating government spending into capital and current expenditure, a better idea is presented of what is the real deficit (current account).

Keynesian Economics

Alan Greenspan

Alan Greenspan was Chairman of the Board of Governors of the Federal Reserve of the United States (or 'Fed') from 1987 to 2006. Prior to his appointment at the Fed, Greenspan was Chairman of the Council of Economic Advisers from 1974 to 1977 under President Gerald Ford.

Born: 1926, New York, USA
Importance: Influential on monetary policy and proponent of laissez-faire capitalism

On 19 October 1987, shortly after taking the Chair at the Fed, Greenspan was faced with a stock market crash, known as Black Monday. This was the second largest one-day percentage decline in the Dow Jones Industrial Average (DJIA) in history. Greenspan, who was to become known for his unique communication style, issued a statement that 'the Fed stands ready to provide all necessary liquidity,' which is viewed as having helped calm the markets.

Greenspan was preceded as Fed chairman by Paul Volcker, who had been confronted with the 'stagflation' of the late 1970s and early 1980s, when the economy was experiencing simultaneous recession and inflation. Under Volcker, the Fed targeted the money supply as the primary variable of monetary policy, but under Greenspan it became accepted that the Fed could not control the money supply; instead, monetary policy became the direct control of two key short-term interest rates. The Federal Funds Rate is the rate of interest member banks of the Federal Reserve system charge one another to borrow reserves. It is also known as the overnight rate or interbank lending rate. The Discount Rate is the rate of interest the Fed charges member banks to borrow reserves from the Fed. The two rates are usually very close to one another, and are benchmark rates that influence other important interest rates, such as the prime rate.

Another famous remark by Greenspan was his reference to 'irrational exuberance and unduly escalating stock prices' on 5 December 1996. The 1990s economic expansion culminated in a bursting of a stock market bubble in March 2000 and an economic recession in 2001–2002. Over 1999 and early 2000, the Federal Reserve had increased interest rates six times in attempting a 'soft landing' of the economy. The Fed later brought interest rates down to historic lows, said to have led to a housing bubble.

One of the important and controversial impacts of the Greenspan era at the Fed was the change in economic priorities. Inflation became 'Public Enemy Number One', and full employment declined in relative importance as a national policy goal. Greenspan was often criticised for using unemployment as a means of controlling inflation. When inflation reared its head, Greenspan would raise interest rates to slow down the economy, causing unemployment to rise and cooling down markets. Greenspan's approach was influential on central banks around the world, who attempted to copy his approach. Nevertheless, during the 1990s boom, Greenspan permitted unemployment to fall to levels below that which was thought to be inflationary. Many observers considered this to prove that it was unnecessary to keep unemployment high to control inflation, and that low unemployment rates were compatible with price stability.

Stagflation: A combination of inflation and recession. It is a problem because most tools used by central bankers for directing the economy trade off growth for inflation; either they slow growth to reduce inflationary pressures, or they allow price increases while generating output growth. Stagflation creates a policy bind in which efforts to correct one problem can worsen the other.

Edmund S. Phelps

Born in Chicago in the midst of the Great Depression, Edmund S. 'Ned' Phelps attended Yale University. He joined the faculty at Columbia University in 1971, where he has remained since, and was appointed the McVickar Professor of Political Economy there in 1982.

Born: 1933, Illinois, USA
Importance: Developed economic growth rate theory
Nobel Prize: 2006

Phelps' contributions have been in a wide variety of areas, most of them employing a 'micro–macro' approach, including unemployment, price stability, monetary theory, expectations and labour market dynamics. He is something of an old-fashioned 'general economist' whose theoretical innovations may be applied in a number of different areas. Some of his best-known work was on the natural rate of unemployment, statistical discrimination theory and – in the area of policy analysis – wage subsidies. Phelps has also been a notable critic of the rational expectations theory and monetary policy rules (such as the currently fashionable applied version of the Taylor rule), where monetary policy is treated as scientific; for Phelps, policy is as much – or even more so – an art.

Statistical discrimination theories were a response to the results of Gary Becker's 'economics of discrimination' model, in which competition and discrimination are incompatible in the long run. This meant that either one had to treat race and gender economic inequalities as resulting from factors other than discrimination (such as differences in productivity, as in the human capital approach), or discard the assumption of perfect competition and resort to models of imperfect competition. The latter was the route taken by statistical discrimination theorists such as Phelps. If the assumption of perfect knowledge were relaxed, for example, and employers do not know the productivity of individual applicants, and it is costly to find this information out, employers may use race or gender as a 'screening device', assuming that individual applicants possess the average productivity of their (race or gender) group, assumed to be lower. Thus, outcomes will appear discriminatory, statistically, and discrimination will also be rational (economically, as in cost-minimising, contrary to Becker's model where employers who discriminate suffer lower profits).

In Phelps' 1997 book *Rewarding Work*, he proposes that government pay firms wage subsidies to promote employment and higher wages for workers. The idea is that some workers can only earn a low wage, if based solely on productivity, so the firm can only pay them a wage that is so high. Many of these workers may prefer not to work for such a low wage under these circumstances, and choose to receive government benefits. If government steps in and subsidises a higher wage, this can draw such workers into the labour market and out of the dole. Thus, employment can increase and dependence on government handouts fall, with workers earning a wage that provides a higher standard of living even while firms only pay what makes economic sense to them. Phelps calculates the costs of such a plan and concludes that it is affordable, given the benefits of higher income and employment.

Paul Krugman

Paul Krugman came to public prominence as a result of his regular column on the op-ed page of the *New York Times*. Krugman graduated from Yale University in 1974 and gained his PhD from Massachusetts Institute of Technology (MIT) three years later. Since 2000, he has been Professor of Economics and International Affairs at Princeton University.

Born: 1953, New York, USA
Importance: Major contributions to international economics especially trade theory

Krugman's economic contributions are primarily notable in the area of international trade. Traditional trade theory, known as the Heckscher-Ohlin-Samuelson (H-O-S) model, makes a number of restricting assumptions, including that markets are perfectly competitive, that trading nations have identical tastes and technologies, that economies are operating at full employment, and that constant returns to scale prevail in production. This last is the proposition that if firms increase all inputs by some equal proportion, output increases by the same proportion.

Krugman began investigating how the results of the analysis would be modified if an economy was characterised by increasing returns to scale (where increasing all inputs by equal proportion results in output increasing by more than that proportion). Industries where increasing returns predominate will tend to have fewer, larger firms and therefore will be better depicted by models of imperfect competition rather than perfect competition.

Another aspect of the increasing returns is the role of expectations. Whether one chooses to use product A over B depends on whether one believes most others will be using product A or not in the future, but whether they will depends on what they believe others will do.

Krugman's main emphasis has been on the importance of geography for economics, part of the 'new economic geography'. The interest is related to the questions of where economic activities take place, why, and the implications. Why do countries closer to the Equator tend to be poor? Why do populations and industry tend to cluster in certain areas and not in others? Krugman's work has combined two approaches to these questions. The first views these outcomes as rooted in underlying geographical conditions, while the second sees these developments as the result of chance events. While some have treated the two approaches as incompatible, Krugman sees them as complementary.

One of the main applications of his theoretical framework has been the economies of agglomeration. This refers to geographical concentrations of population and activity in general. The primary explanation for agglomeration has been the existence of increasing returns, which also means imperfect competition. There are important implications of this work for trade theory, such as explaining regional specialisation and trade in an alternative manner from the traditional theory of comparative advantage. Thus, the various streams of Krugman's thought – trade theory, economic geography, increasing returns and imperfect competition – come together to have an impact on mainstream economics.

Consumer Behaviour

Consumption spending by individuals and households is a
powerful motor of a market economy. Investors take expectations
of future expenditure by consumers as a very important signal for
planning their capacity and production. Wall Street and the City
pay careful attention to consumer confidence, which can be very
fickle. Luxury spending cannot drive a large industrial economy;
mass production must serve mass consumption.

The early Neoclassical authors shifted the focus of economics
away from production, which had been of prime concern for the
classical authors, and towards consumption. Consumer behaviour
was described by the theory of choice, where consumer
preferences were guided by the principles of utility maximisation,
including the law of diminishing marginal utility (the idea that we
receive less *additional* utility from each successive unit of a
particular good).

The contributions of institutional economists to the theory of
consumer behaviour are similar to the direction that modern
economics has taken, with a little help from psychology and
sociology. Veblen's notion of 'conspicuous consumption', for
example, challenged the notion that consumers do not affect one
another's preferences. In *The Theory of the Leisure Class* (1899),
Veblen wrote of the ways in which the wealthy displayed their
economic and social power through expensive and largely useless
decoration and dressing.

Some consumers purchase certain goods in order to be 'part
of the crowd', so consumption becomes a way of expressing one's
social position and relations. This type of behaviour has been
termed the 'bandwagon effect'. In other cases, individual
consumption decisions will be driven by a desire to distinguish

oneself from the crowd, exhibiting the 'snob effect'. Interestingly, the snob effect does not always mean driving the fanciest car or wearing designer jeans. It can also mean driving the most beat-up looking automobile or wearing the most faded or ripped up jeans.

Sometimes such behaviour can even violate the laws of economics. What has sometimes been termed the 'Veblen effect' is a situation in which the demand curve can be upward sloping, meaning the higher the price the higher the demand for the good, violating the 'law of demand' (normally, lower prices mean more demand and higher prices mean lower demand). People may buy more expensive goods to show that they can afford them. Another source of the upward-sloping demand curve is when individuals use price as an indicator of quality (think of when a good is priced so low that it is 'too good to be true', in other words, there must be something wrong with it).

Newer approaches to consumer behaviour replace the maximising assumption, where more is always better than less, with the notion of 'satisficing', or that enough is better. The notions of procedural and bounded rationality are alternatives to the traditional global rationality assumption. The theory of procedural rationality emphasises rules, habits, social norms, rules of thumb and recommendations from others in making consumption decisions. Keynes claimed that his notion of the 'marginal propensity to consume' (the additional spending resulting from an additional dollar of income) was a 'psychological law', and James Duesenberry later proposed the 'relative income hypothesis,' emphasising emulation, which harks back to Veblen and the Institutionalists.

Gustav von Schmoller

Gustav Schmoller was one of Germany's leading economists and Professor at the University of Berlin, at that time the most important university in Europe. Schmoller founded the German Economic Association and was hugely influential in the arena of economic and fiscal reform. Schmoller revived a school of economic analysis that came to be known as the German Historical School. The School's main emphasis was the importance of historical context and institutions in the analysis of complex socio-economic phenomena.

Born: 1838, Heibronn, Germany
Importance: The leader of the 'younger' German historical school of economics
Died: 1917, Bad Harzburg, Germany

In order to understand the significance of the German Historical School we need to recall that at the turn of the twentieth century, conventional economic theory commonly relied on the deductive method of analysis. 'Economic laws' were deduced from assumptions about how humans act in pursuit of their economic interests. For example, a self-regulating economy with a harmony of interests emerged from the assumption of an 'economic man' who was guided purely by self-interest. Historical context and institutions did not matter in such analysis because the 'laws' of economic life were universal and undeniable, and would therefore hold under any historical conditions.

German Historicism realised the fallacy of the conventional approach and developed its own alternative – a historical method of analysis that Schmoller described in the *Outline of General Economcis* (1904).

Schmoller was convinced that economic theory should be embedded in the analysis of institutions because institutions shape human behaviour, including their economic behaviour. Economic action cannot be understood solely from fixed assumptions about human nature because this action is guided to a large extent by existing customs, traditions and institutions within a society.

Schmoller argued that the only way to study complex socio-economic phenomena was to look at their historical developments and study causal effects, as opposed to the study of static, universal and abstract theory that conventional economics proposed. Moreover, he argued economics cannot be viewed in isolation from other aspects of real life. Only a concrete historical inquiry into economic, social, political and cultural factors and their interrelatedness can give a thorough understanding of present economic conditions. Reason and deductive logic alone cannot grasp the complex underlying reality.

He dismissed the concept of a self-regulating economy with a prevailing harmony of interests. On the contrary, he saw conflict between social classes and believed this called for resolution by state intervention and social reform.

Development of economics through historical and social perceptions ensures the discipline is relevant and useful for solving complex socio-economic problems and the methods of the German Historical School made a lasting contribution on economics and, more particularly, social science.

German Historical School: This school of historical thought believed that history was the key source of knowledge about human actions and economic matters, as economics is culture-specific and therefore cannot be generalised. It was interested in the realities of economics and how this affected humans, rather than in abstract mathematical models.

Chartalism

Georg Friedrich Knapp

At the beginning of the twentieth century, countries throughout the world were debating the optimal metallic standard for their monetary systems. Georg Friedrich Knapp, a member of the German Historical School, suggested that there was no need for a metallic standard for a currency at all. He argued that money need not be backed by a commodity with an intrinsic value. Money instead could be chartal (modern or state) money.

Born: 1842, Giessen, Germany
Importance: Argued for the introduction of a chartalist system of money
Died: 1926, Darmstadt, Germany

The term 'chartal' derives from the Greek 'chartes', the word for the leaf of the papyrus plant, or a sheet of paper, or something on which to make marks. By chartal money, Knapp was referring to any money whose exchange value exceeds its intrinsic value. He argued that the 'means of payment' became 'money' not because the means held intrinsic value in itself, but because it had been chartered by the state and declared acceptable in payment of taxes at public pay offices.

Knapp explained that originally coins were minted by the state as an alternative to collecting taxes in kind. Minting created a uniform medium for the payment of taxes and thus facilitated the fiscal relationship between the state and its subjects. Here we can see a close link between money creation and taxation within the sovereignty of the state. The public demanded the state's money because that was the form in which taxes had to be paid.

The state would mint coins and pay them out for the goods and services provided by the private sector. Then, the state would collect those coins in payment of taxes and other obligations. The state thus used taxes as a means of inducing its citizens to provide

98 99

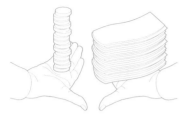

goods and services, supplying in return the money in which tax liabilities would be paid.

When metals became too rare for the expanding economies, paper money substituted the minted coins. Thus money became devoid of any intrinsic value in itself. Neither was it backed by assets with intrinsic value. Money became a ticket, a chartal piece that represented a measure of value and was used in payment of taxes to the state.

Chartalism is opposed to the metallist view on the nature and evolution of money. The former isolates the theory of money from the theory of the state and traces the origin of money to the sphere of private exchange, where the means of payment with minimal transaction costs became money. The metallist approach emphasises the intrinsic value of money or of the asset that backs it. The metallic money standard became obsolete in the post-Bretton Woods era after 1944, when money was backed not by gold, but by the sovereign power of the state.

Robert L. Heilbroner

Robert Louis Heilbroner was an economist and public intellectual best known for his popular book *The Worldly Philosophers* (1953), in which he outlined the dramatic scenarios of the Classical political economists. The classical scenarios depict the almost inexorable movement of the capitalist economic system, with its 'laws of motion' and its systematic tendencies leading to some 'future immanent in the present'.

Born: 1919, New York, USA
Importance: Integrated ideas from history, economics, and philosophy
Died: 2005, New York, USA

Heilbroner argued that the trajectory of the capitalist system is inseparable from both the wider sociopolitical context within which the economy is situated, and the subjective drives and behavioural tendencies of historical agents, which both shape and are shaped by changing socioeconomic and political structures.

Heilbroner's initial fascination with the worldly philosophers' prognoses led to his own analyses of the economic, political, cultural, and sociopsychological motivations and propensities underlying production, distribution, and exchange. In these investigations, Heilbroner adopted his own versions of Joseph Schumpeter's notions of 'vision' and 'analysis'. Whereas for Schumpeter analysis had a kind of 'cleansing' effect that prevented the necessarily ideological nature of the 'pre-analytical cognitive act' from tainting the scientific endeavor, for Heilbroner economic theory was inescapably value-laden: biases are always present, at times lurking just beneath the surface, but often emerging in the form of assumptions that determine the content of analytical categories and the direction of prognostications.

Although Heilbroner's explicit self-identification with a 'hermeneutic' (interpretive) approach came relatively late, he had always emphasized that inquiry necessarily has an interpretive dimension. For Heilbroner, this meant that the very object of inquiry cannot be presumed self-evident. The 'economy' is an abstraction from the social totality, and thus defining the subject matter of economics is a task that influences the nature and direction of analysis. Heilbroner long advocated 'material provisioning' – the harnessing of society's material resources to provide for the needs and wants of its members – as the central problematic of the political economist. He thus argued against any notion of universal economic 'laws', emphasizing the historical specificity of capitalism in human history. Heilbroner's historical approach, rejection of universal laws, and refusal to 'read' markets back into precapitalist societies provided a welcome respite from the 'economics imperialism' of modern Neoclassical economics.

In later years, Heilbroner questioned whether, under present contemporary circumstances, worldly philosophy is still possible. He believed that scenarios and visions do not lend themselves to formal analytical procedures. More importantly, he held the position that the economic behaviours that set the system on its path have become less dependable, while political intervention has become more strategic. An 'instrumental' approach thus becomes more appropriate, with 'blueprints depicting possible routes from present realities to desired destinations' replacing 'scenarios depicting a future immanent in the present' (*The Crisis of Vision in Modern Economic Thought*, 1996).

Peter Kropotkin

Russian social and political philosopher and one of the foremost speakers of the anarchist movement, Peter Kropotkin saw anarchism as a product of the class struggle against capitalism and the state. He developed a coherent theory of anarchic communism and wrote a number of books, such as *Modern Science and Anarchism* (1908), *Mutual Aid: a Factor in Evolution* (1902) and *Fields, Factories and Workshops* (1912), that made a significant contribution to the evolution of the theory of anarchism.

Born: 1842, Moscow, Russia
Importance: Developed a coherent theory of anarchic communism.
Died: 1921, Dmitrov, Moscow, Russia

Kropotkin's anarcho-communism involved opposition towards both the state and capitalism. He saw anarchism as a result of the everyday class struggle, specifically the struggle of workers against exploitation by capitalists and oppression and domination by the state. Capitalism seeks centralisation in order to empower and enrich the few. Kropotkin saw decentralised cooperation in society within a federation of free self-managing communes as a preferred form of social organisation.

Anarchists claim that communities can enjoy the benefits of increased productivity from specialisation without the negative effects the division of labour has on workers, by permitting individuals to alternate between the various assignments.

In an anarcho-communist society, harmony and order would be achieved not by submission to the law or by obedience to the authority, but through free agreements concluded between the various groups. Such a society would go through ever-changing adjustments and readjustments that would be easier to withstand if government did not interfere in the process.

In his famous book, *Mutual Aid*, Kropotkin insisted that cooperation and mutual aid were the norms in both the natural and social worlds. He argued that a major factor in the evolutionary success of mankind was a predisposition to cooperate and to share, without the need for institutions such as the market or the state. Kropotkin argued that cooperation was a primary survival strategy for humans. From this perspective he developed a theory of social organisation in his *Fields, Factories and Workshops* that was based upon communes of producers linked with each other through common custom and free contract.

Anarchism: Literally means 'the absence of the state'. In a broader sense, anarchism is defined as a form of social organisation where there is no place for the government.

In his *Modern Science and Anarchism*, Kropotkin attempted to put anarchism on scientific grounds. As a distinguished natural scientist he derived many of his political beliefs from his studies of human and animal evolution. He was well acquainted with the methods of scientific inquiry and stressed the importance of applying the inductive-deductive method for the analysis of everyday society in order to build a scientific theory of anarchism.

Kropotkin also paid particular attention to issues regarding the division of labour. He opposed the division between manual and intellectual labour, claiming that all society's members need the opportunity to engage in both physical and mental work. In addition, Kropotkin also opposed the division between the 'field' and the 'workshop', again proposing that all individuals require the chance to operate in both settings.

Thorstein Veblen

An enigmatic figure in the history of economics, Thorstein Veblen's work reflects the fact that he lived and wrote during the second industrial revolution (approximately 1871–1914), a period characterised by great technological advances, development of mass production and separation of ownership from management in industrial enterprises.

Born: 1857, Wisconsin, USA
Importance: A sociologist and economist and a leader of the Efficiency Movement
Died: 1929, California, USA

It was clear to Veblen that static economic theory could not account for the continuously changing socio-economic order. He argued that the subject matter of economics should be the study of institutions in their evolutionary character (that is, as their nature evolves over time). In contrast, conventional economic theory was concerned with the formulation of unchangeable economic laws.

In his attempt to identify the what, the how and the why of socio-economic change, Veblen outlined two major factors: technology and institutions. Technological advance was an impetus to change, whereas existing social institutions were backward, binding protectors of the status quo. Together, the opposing forces of institutions and technology determined the nature of socio-economic and cultural change. Veblen's theoretical approach became the foundation of the new framework of economic analysis called Institutional Economics.

The Institutional school of thought was propelled by various followers of Veblen beyond America to other countries around the globe. The main characteristics of the school are a suspicion of highly abstract theory not grounded in reality, and a continuous emphasis on historical and empirical relevance.

At the same time, Veblen was a pungent social critic. He is perhaps best known for his theory of conspicuous consumption and in his *Theory of the Leisure Class* (1899) showed that pecuniary or money-related emulation played a crucial role in consumer behaviour. Conspicuous displays of consumption and leisure were a means to demonstrate one's monetary superiority. Within such a social context, an ongoing demonstration of personal wealth was the key to social esteem and emulation.

Veblen coined the term 'pecuniary instincts' to demonstrate how strong the wealth struggle was in humans. However, pecuniary instinct was not the sole driving force behind human behaviour. In his famous work *The Instinct of Workmanship and the Irksomeness of Labour* (1914), Veblen characterised humans as endowed with the so-called 'instinct' of workmanship. This concept holds that monetary reward is not the only motive inducing people to work. On the contrary, Veblen argued, aside from pecuniary gains, work gives people a sense of gratification in performing useful tasks. Unfortunately, businessmen were no longer guided by the instinct of workmanship since their pecuniary instincts superseded it.

In his analysis of enterprise, Veblen became famous for his distinction between business and industry, first made in 1904 in the *Theory of Business Enterprise*. Business was all about money and profit-making, whereas industry was distinguished by workmanship, social serviceability of the product and innovation.

Veblen noticed how the separation of ownership from management in industrial enterprises was detrimental to the serviceability of the product to the community. The everyday operations of business entities were overseen by managers for whom the job was meaningless since their ability to undertake individual initiative and hence the instincts of workmanship were thwarted.

Business Cycle Theory

Business cycles are continuous patterns of short-term, cyclical economic expansion and contraction. Business cycle theory became most prominent during the Great Depression – the years between the First and Second World Wars – during which time the causes of and cures for recessions and depressions were hotly debated.

Historically, business cycles have differed in terms of the economic factors that made up their movements. In the nineteenth century, the price level would rise during expansions and fall during contractions; throughout the twentieth century, the price level rose steadily but output and employment would rise during booms and fall during slumps. There are also such things as 'growth recessions', in which there is a fall in the rate of growth of output and employment, but growth does not actually turn negative.

Many different theories have been put forward to explain the business cycle. Most attempt to identify the factor or factors that directly or indirectly regulate investment. Among the candidates are theories that focus on monetary factors, such as the banking system and monetary policy, and those that rooted the cycles in technological change.

There are a number of different monetary theories, but all view the cycle as the result of money and credit, the banking system or monetary policy. Knut Wicksell's theory, which held that the difference between the bank rate of interest and the natural or normal rate of interest led to expansions or contractions in the demand for credit, influenced many later monetary approaches to the business cycle. Ludwig von Mises, Friedrich Hayek and the Austrian school emphasised bad monetary policy, which resulted in interest rates that misled investors, thus affecting the capital structure of the economy. Keynes emphasised investor expectations being subject to waves of optimism and pessimism, and the economic impact of the 'flight to liquidity' (when investors eschew what they perceive as high-risk investments in favor of more liquid ones) – the increased demand for money.

In contrast, technological theories of the business cycle did not believe that monetary disturbances were at the root of a crisis, but rather that they simply exacerbated the problem. In this approach, growth and the cycle itself are seen to be caused by the same phenomena, whereas in the monetary approach growth and cycles are explained differently. Schumpeter viewed cycles as rooted in swarms of technological innovation, which then also affected growth. Other authors of this persuasion argued that competition compelled firms to introduce labour-saving technological innovations – in other words, that the causes of the cycle are endogenous, or determined by market forces.

Policy approaches to the problems caused by the business cycle range from those that see government intervention as ineffective, to those that view either monetary or fiscal policy as the more important approach. Contemporary stabilisation policies have included jobs programmes, incomes policies and other approaches to complement traditional fiscal and monetary policies. Some of these policy options are intended to address not only the aggregate imbalances, but also the sectoral issues involved in the business cycle.

Karl Wilhelm (William) Kapp

European institutional economist Karl William Kapp devoted his life to the economic analysis of socio-ecological disruption and degradation resulting from the unfettered operation of businesses. Regardless of the form of ownership (private, state and so on), Kapp argued that enterprise would cause negative socio-ecological effects due to its cost-minimising nature.

Born: 1910, Konigsberg, Germany

Importance: Identified the importance of recognising the social costs of economic activity

Died: 1976, Dubrovnik, Croatia

Environmental pollution through the production and disposal of waste, deforestation and soil degradation caused by agricultural practices, disruption of ecological balance, depletion of natural resources, occupational diseases, exposure to radiation, unemployment due to labour-saving capital-intensive production activities and many other adverse effects on the environment and people's health and welfare are all examples of social costs that impinge upon present and future generations.

Kapp identified these costs as *social* because they are not paid for by those responsible for them, and are shifted instead to third parties or society at whole. In the case of environmental disruption and pollution, social costs result not only from the reluctance of those responsible for them to pay, but also from the problem of identifying the initial polluter's share in the environmental damage, the extent of the damage, the number of people affected by it and the degree of the effect.

This is made more difficult because the effects of pollution may become evident only several years after the initial act of pollution took place. The fact that the pollution process is cumulative also complicates matters, because the magnitude of the initial effect is amplified through self-reinforcement and interaction with other pollutants through time. How these costs will be divided among hundreds and thousands of enterprises over long periods of time is a difficult issue to resolve.

The problem of integrating social costs into the current trends of economic analysis lies also with determination of their market value. The qualitative nature of social costs questions the applicability of monetary cost accounting. How do we determine market values on things like health, life and nature?

If we cannot identify the source and spread of social costs, and if we cannot measure them appropriately in monetary terms, then we cannot outline a market policy of fully internalizing them. This enables the firms to shift these costs of production to society or future generations, thus decreasing their production costs, increasing revenues and appropriating a larger share of the national income. Today's consumers purchase the goods at less than the full price; the producers did not bear the full cost of production, as part of it took the form of social costs.

Kapp argued that the only way to solve the issue of social costs would be to implement a different decision-making process as regards technology, production and investment *before* the social costs occur. If such practice were operationalised, all those affected by social costs would have a voice. Such decision making would be based on a social evaluation process of the possible costs (such as pollution effects) and benefits (such as employment) related to the investment decision. The most important objective criteria for this kind of decision making would be to secure the social minima – clean air and water and other objective human needs such as food, housing, health care, education and security. With the provision of such social minima requirements, investors could no longer put at risk conditions for long-term ecological and social reproduction in the pursuit of their profit interests.

John Kenneth Galbraith

Harvard economist J. K. Galbraith challenged the 'conventional wisdom'. Born and raised on a Canadian farm, Galbraith studied agricultural economics at the University of California, Berkeley and then accepted a teaching position at Harvard University, where he remained for his entire career. He was a sceptic regarding the beneficence of markets, and an unapologetic proponent of government regulation of the economy.

Born: 1908, Ontario, Canada
Importance: A proponent of regulation of the economy by the government
Died: 2006, Massachusetts, USA

At a time when the economics profession was moving toward ever more formal, mathematical models, Galbraith was squarely in the political economy tradition of the old Classical economists, as well as Marx, Keynes, Schumpeter and Veblen. Galbraith's first important policy position was in the Office of Price Administration during the Second World War. Later he advised President John F. Kennedy, who appointed him Ambassador to India in 1961. Although often critical of his profession, Galbraith was respected by his colleagues, who elected him President of the American Economic Association in 1972. A prolific writer, his most famous works include *The Great Crash: 1929* (1955), *The Affluent Society* (1958), *The New Industrial State* (1967) and *Economics and the Public Purpose* (1973).

Galbraith arrived at Harvard in the midst of both the Keynesian revolution in macroeconomics and the monopolistic competition revolution in microeconomics. He became an eloquent proponent of post-Keynesian policies aimed at promoting full employment, and he criticized conventional economic theory for failing to account for modern developments within a capitalist economy during the era of the giant corporations. The system of small competitive enterprise was increasingly confronted with the giant enterprises enjoying a high degree of market power. Contrary to conventional wisdom, huge corporations could exert control over prices as well as over consumers through advertising methods. Galbraith rejected the conventional, informative function attributed to advertising, arguing instead that advertising manipulated consumers by creating artificial needs which firms then aimed to satisfy. He attacked the Neoclassical notion of consumer sovereignty and replaced it by producer sovereignty.

In order to prevent this, 'countervailing power' (another term coined by Galbraith) was necessary. Consumer organisations, trades unions, and government intervention could assist in preventing the dangers arising from the deregulated oligopolistic markets.

Galbraith used the term 'planning system' to refer to the competitive market forces characteristic of nineteenth-century entrepreneurial capitalism. Galbraith was an evolutionist in his thinking. He maintained that the Neoclassical theory was applicable to a free market economy, whereas the planning system of modern corporations did not fit into this theoretical framework. The planning system of modern corporations had most of the wealth and power and was responsible for its uneven distribution. The failure of Neoclassical economics to address the issues of power struggle became Galbraith's life-long theme. He continuously stressed the importance of power and power relations in understanding modern capitalism.

Charlotte Perkins Gilman

Charlotte Perkins Gilman was a self-educated economic sociologist and social critic, playwright, novelist and poet. She was the forerunner in arguing that women's increasing part in the labour force would not only liberate women, but also be good for the economy. Gilman brought attention to the important role of household labour in an economy and predicted that many of the activities traditionally associated with unpaid housework and child rearing would evolve into market-based services.

Born: 1860, Connecticut, USA
Importance: Brought an awareness of gender issues into the study of economics
Died: 1935, Pasadena, USA

Her most famous work on economics is *Women and Economics* (1898). Regarded by many as the mother of feminist economics, Gilman believed that gender inequality was the result of institutional structure, not biological factors. Institutional change could alter gender-economic relations and both improve the lot of women and benefit society at large. Her argument was based on the economic principle that specialisation increases efficiency and output. Freed from institutionally enforced dependence on men, women could excel in the labour market, and housework would become more efficient.

Gilman proposed egalitarian marriages, emphasising the increase in efficiency benefitting both women and men and the increased market provision of home-based activities. Influenced by Darwin, Gilman viewed human evolution as, in part, socially determined, in particular by planned institutions. She was thus something of a socialist, but with a faith in market solutions, and her work has family resemblances to that of her contemporary, Thorstein Veblen.

Both Neoclassical and Marxian approaches have been criticised for their 'gender-blindness', masking the male-centred nature of their frameworks. Giving privilege to paid market work over unpaid household labour is an example of gender-biased economics. Occupational segregation and gender wage differentials became topics of theoretical and empirical investigation. The Neoclassical theories of discrimination, including those initially geared at racial economic inequality, were applied to gender relations. Others moved in a more philosophical and interdisciplinary direction, following the lead of Women's Studies and feminist scholarship more generally. Gender also became an important area of study in development economics, with the extension of the Human Development Index to account for gender differences (GDI, or Gender-related Development Index) and the rise of Gender and Development as a field of study. Black and Third World feminism have questioned the class and race biases in Western feminist approaches, and ecological feminists have linked the issues of gender and the environment. Feminist economics may have emerged in the 1980s, with the culmination of work begun in the 1960s on patriarchy and gender economic inequality, but the movement has always recognised its debt to Gilman.

'We are the only animal species in which the female depends on the male for food, the only animal species in which the sex-relation is also an economic relation. With us an entire sex lives in a relation of economic dependence upon the other sex, and the economic relation is combined with the sex-relation'.

Women and Economics

Simon Kuznets

The American economist and Nobel Prize winner Simon Kuznets is best known for his study of income growth and inequality, national income accounting, theory of economic development and growth and the theory of business cycles. Often called 'the father of national income accounting', Kuznets emphasised the complexity of the underlying economic and social reality, and the importance of empirical research for economic analysis.

Born: 1901, Kharkov, Ukraine
Importance: Major contributions to economic growth theories
Nobel Prize: 1971
Died: 1985, Massachusetts, USA

Kuznets was elected President of the American Economic Association in 1954 and, together with Wesley C. Mitchell, he worked at the National Bureau of Economic Research to develop the standardised measurement of gross national product (GNP).

Kuznets identified the inverted U-shaped relation between income inequality and economic growth ('Kuznets's curve'). This hypothesis states that in the course of economic development, as measured by growth of real per capita GNP, the size distribution of personal income will be unequal at first, will stabilise gradually, and then become more equal. Therefore, income inequality had to rise before it could become more equal.

His original hypothesis was derived from Kuznets's examination of the historical experience of presently developed nations, which showed that, at the very low levels of per capita GNP, great inequality was limited by the minimal subsistence requirements of individuals on the lowest incomes. As growth took place, the concentration of savings among upper-income groups, and a tendency toward a shift in the industrial structure of the labour force away from agriculture toward manufacturing,

Inequality

Income per capita

Left: Kuznets curve shows that income equality stabilizes as GNP increases.

initially caused an increase in relative inequality. As growth continued, certain counter-forces resulted in decreased inequality. In particular, Kuznets attributed this to legislative factors, such as inheritance taxes, and to demographic factors that resulted in relative population decrease within the upper-income groups, as well as toward factors relating to social and technological change.

Kuznets recognised the major differences between the underdeveloped countries of his day, and the pre-industrial stages through which contemporary developed nations had evolved. Such differences suggested to him much greater obstacles to the economic development and growth in contemporary underdeveloped countries. Despite Kuznets' own warnings to the contrary, some took his hypothesis to support the view that developing economies should focus only on growth, and not be concerned with income distribution.

More recent work demonstrating rising inequality in many OECD (Organisation for Economic Co-operation and Development) countries since 1980 encourages more subtle and complex political-economic analyses than that of the simple relationship between economic growth and income inequality. As Kuznets would be the first to admit, a nation's development is not determined solely by internal factors in isolation, and careful examination of the global context is crucial to considerations of both economic growth and income distribution.

Development Economics

Nicholas Georgescu-Roegen

Nicholas Georgescu-Roegen is known as the founder of ecological or bio-economics. Born in a peasant community in Romania, he became a brilliant mathematician and worked extensively on the bio-physical foundations of economics. Linking economics, environment and social reality together, Georgescu-Roegen was concerned with entropy and bio-degradation of the environment due to the economic process. His *The Entropy Law and the Economic Process* (1971) became the foundations of the contemporary school of ecological economics.

Born: 1906, Constanta, Romania
Importance: Introduced the concept of entropy from thermodynamics
Died: 1994, Tennessee, USA

The implications of the laws of thermodynamics to economics are the core of Georgescu-Roegen's approach. In a finite environment, the economic process is only possible by depleting the finite stocks of natural resources that serve as inputs into the production process. Exponential growth, so avowed by traditional economics, is thus not possible. Not only growth, but a zero-growth state cannot exist forever in a finite environment. The consequences of the laws of thermodynamics are that the economy must shrink. Unlimited growth is not possible due to the bio-physical constraints of the environment. Even solar energy is not a solution because the entropic

'From the purely physical viewpoint, the economic process is entropic: it neither creates nor consumes matter or energy, but only transforms low into high entropy [that is, irrevocable waste].'

Georgescu-Roegen,
Analytical Economics, 1966

degradation of mineral resources may prove even more crucial than entropic degradation of energy. The depletion of mineral resources and energy must therefore be as small as feasible.

Georgescu-Roegen emphasised the issues of intergenerational inequality in the usage of resources. Economic activity of the present generation has an impact on the economic activities of future generations as energy and materials in the finite environment are irrevocably used up and the harmful effects of pollution on the environment accumulate. However, with the monopoly of present over future generations, future generations don't have a say in this process.

Technological progress in a finite natural environment cannot materialise forever unless the corresponding technological innovation is followed by major mineralogical discoveries. The direction of technological innovation should be carried out towards ecologically viable methods of production and energy generation.

Georgescu-Roegen emphasised the role that the demand side of the economy could play in sustaining the environment, by moderating consumption and avoiding waste. Humans have a choice. They can either deplete the available stocks of useful resources as soon as they can, or they can reduce their material standards of living and thus protract the live spans of future generations. Humans should get rid of their short-sightedness and perceive themselves as part of the evolving organism – human species – and not as atomistic selfish consumers.

Thermodynamics:
The first law of thermodynamics states that energy can neither be created nor destroyed, it can only change in form. The second law (the entropy law), states that any utilisation of energy decreases the total amount of useful energy available for future use. Georgescu-Roegen emphasised that it is not only energy, but matter too, that is subject to entropic degradation.

Economic Development

Development indicates economic growth, but it is almost always intended to indicate qualitative as well as quantitative social and economic advancement. The Classical authors are usually thought to have put forward theories of economic development, and the term was also associated with studies by later figures such as Joseph Schumpeter. In the post-Second World War period, the field of economic development is most often used with reference to the developing countries of Asia, Africa and the Americas.

In the early days of the discipline, it was generally agreed that policies appropriate for industrialised nations, especially the Keynesian policies then in fashion, were not applicable to the developing world. Keynes' theories assumed a nation had a significant amount of unused capacity as well as labour unemployment, so expansionary fiscal and monetary policies were intended to increase employment and the utilisation of capacity. Developing countries had surplus labour, but they did not possess the capacity, and so capital formation was required.

One focus of early development economics was the peculiar conditions facing developing nations, mostly stemming from their former colonial status. During colonialism, the mother country exploited the resources of the colonies and paid little attention to the conditions for balanced growth. As a result, most developing countries suffered from a lack of sectoral integration within their own economies, which were often structured for producing one or few export crops or natural resources for the industrialised world. This made them vulnerable to swings in global commodity prices and falling terms of trade between manufactured goods and primary products (for example, it would take more and more cocoa to purchase the same amount of radios).

The United Nations has played an important role in promoting economic development. In particular, the United Nations Conference on Trade and Development (UNCTAD) and the United Nations Development Program (UNDP) conduct a considerable amount of research related to development planning and policy formation, as well as overseeing and arranging funding for many projects. Many important economists have worked through the United Nations on development issues, including Raul Prebisch and, more recently, Amartya Sen, whose contributions to the Human Development Index have been utilised in a number of studies.

Other international agencies, such as the World Bank and the International Monetary Fund (IMF), have considerable influence on economic development. Among these agencies, the emphasis in the latter part of the twentieth century was switched from government intervention to market-based policies, embodied in structural adjustment programs (SAPs). These included balancing budgets, tax cuts, cuts in government spending, deregulation and other policies geared toward freeing up the market and free trade.

While these schemes have had some success in promoting economic development, global poverty, inequality and unemployment remain troubling concerns, especially in Africa, where health problems such as the AIDS crisis constitute considerable obstacles. In addition, the failure to increase living standards has given rise to social and political instability in many regions, sapping resources and further blocking progress.

Joseph Schumpeter

Moravian-born Austrian-American economist Joseph Alois
Schumpeter was one of the greatest theorists of economic
development and business cycles. He is best known for his
theories on Creative Destruction.

Born: 1883, Trest, Austria-
Hungary (now Czech
Republic)
Importance: Major
contributions to business
cycle theory and dynamic
economics
Died: 1950, Harvard, USA

The idea of the business cycle itself is a view that
economic growth is not gradual and continuous, but
a wave-like dynamic process of alternating cycles of
growth and stagnation. Schumpeter was one of those
economists who set themselves to discover the
driving forces behind these cycles and economic
development generally. His major ideas on economic
dynamics are expressed in *The Theory of Economic
Development* (1911) and *Business Cycles* (1939).

Schumpeter concluded that the major driving
force disrupting the stationary state of the economy
was technological progress (or innovation). Innovations exist on
various scales, such as local, regional, national or global markets;
with varying effects over time. They give impulses for change and
thus disrupt the stationary state of the economy. Once the
innovation proves to be successful and becomes dispersed, the
system again settles in the stationary, until the next round of
innovation takes place. Schumpeter saw entrepreneurs as the ones
who brought innovations into markets as they were continuously
seeking better profit opportunities. As their creative energies were
central to the drive of the economy, entrepreneurs were of
primary interest to Schumpeter and at the central stage of his
analysis of economic growth.

Schumpeter replaced the conventional concept of price
competition with the notion of competition in innovation. Instead

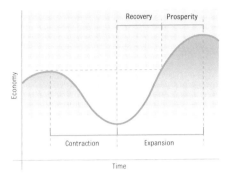

Recovery | Prosperity

Economy

Contraction | Expansion

Time

Left: Business cycle theory explains the cyclical nature of economic contraction and expansion.

of competing in terms of price, firms compete by bringing new competitive products to the markets, improving the quality of existing products, offering new services, etc. Even monopolies and oligopolies have the threat of innovation hanging over them.

Schumpeter identified five major categories of innovation. Product innovations bring new or improved goods or services into the market. Process innovations introduce improved techniques into production processes. The opening up of new markets creates novel opportunities for sales and growth. Discovering alternative supplies of natural resources will support the system's requirements for growth. Finally, organisational innovations will increase productivity and affect allocation of labour among the sectors of the economy. All of these types of innovation may be operating at the same time and can interact in various ways.

Schumpeter's theory of money, credit and financial system was also important to his overall vision. Entrepreneurs cannot afford to fully finance innovation out of their business savings. Promotion of market innovation therefore requires a banking system with credit-creation powers and affordable credit terms.

Creative destruction:
A term famously coined by Schumpeter for the effect on markets of new and improved technology that takes the place of existing products and technologies and renders them obsolete. A marketplace can be turned upside-down by the adoption of new patterns of production and consumption.

Development Economics

Wassily Leontief

Wassily Leontief developed modern input–output (I–O) analysis, an indispensable tool for economic analysis and policy, for which he was awarded the Nobel Memorial Prize in 1973. In addition, Leontief applied the input–output framework in areas such as international trade, technological unemployment and environmental economics.

Born: 1906, Munich, Germany
Importance: Developed input–output analysis
Died: 1999, New York, USA

Russian-born, Leontief attended his home town University of St. Petersburg, which by the time he graduated in 1925, age 19, had been renamed Leningrad. He moved to Germany and became part of the 'Kiel School' of economics, a group that referred to Quesnay's *Tableau Economique* and Marx's reproduction schemes for inspiration in modeling intersectoral relations in industrial capitalist economies. In 1928, Leontief received his doctorate from the University of Berlin and subsequently became Professor at Harvard University. By 1975 he was director of the Institute of Economic Analysis in New York.

Leontief was an admirer of Walras who sought to revive the Classical frameworks of Ricardo and Marx in the light of the Walrasian system. What Leontief did was turn the anonymous markets and perfectly divisible goods of general equilibrium into real sectors with fixed technical coefficients of production. Input–output tables reveal the structure of industrial production in the economy, where outputs are also inputs, direct and indirect, into the production of other goods, and sometimes even inputs in their own production. I–O analysis also reveals the technological structure of production, in terms of factors such as the technological make-up of capital goods, labour productivity, the capital–labour ratios in various sectors, and so on.

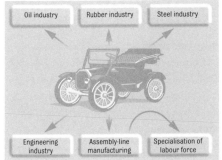

Oil industry | Rubber industry | Steel industry

Engineering industry | Assembly-line manufacturing | Specialisation of labour force

Left: The development of one industry, such as the invention of the automobile, can have a galvanising effect on many seeminly unrelated industries.

Multisectoral models of large size are particularly useful for real world analysis and policy formulation, including economic planning. Leontief was a supporter of indicative planning, used by the French and Japanese in the post-war period. In indicative planning, rather than a planning board fixing all prices and quantities, only a select few are set in key industries, so as to influence the wider economy via market mechanisms.

One of the many useful properties of the input–output framework is the ability to demonstrate the economy-wide impact of waves of technical innovation. For example, a major innovation such as the railroad or the automobile would stimulate or even give rise to many other sectors directly and indirectly, and those sectors would in turn stimulate others. As well, new technologies also displace others, which may result in the demise of sectors, and so on. This all reflects the ways in which I–O analysis maps structural change in the economy.

Despite the mathematical character of his own work, Leontief warned that unrealistic assumptions threatened to reduce the practical relevance of economic science.

Amartya Sen

Amartya Sen was awarded the Nobel Memorial Prize in Economics in 1998 for his research on the development of human capabilities and the alleviation of economic hardship that can impede human potential: poverty, inequality, unemployment and malnutrition. A major aspect of his work has been the development of alternative indicators for measuring human development.

Born: 1933, Santiniketan, India
Importance: Influential work on public choice, human development and welfare economics
Nobel Prize: 1998

Sen's search for an alternative to use of GDP as an economic measure led to the development of his 'capabilities approach' and the Human Development Index (HDI). Individual and social well-being is not simply a matter of consuming goods and services and the HDI includes not only GDP, but also life expectancy and educational attainment in its calculation. Several versions of the HDI have been formulated, to account for issues such as gender and racial/ethnic disparities and income distribution. The focus on inequality follows Sen's proposition that relative inequalities may impact absolute capabilities.

This basic approach has affected Sen's work in other areas. In discussing employment, Sen has proposed that there are three important aspects: employment provides income for the employed; produces goods and services for society; and earns the employed the recognition that they are contributing to community by engaging in a worthwhile activity. The first two aspects have been commonly recognised, but the third is also crucial. This insight is backed up by research on unemployment and clinical depression, demonstrating that the issues not only apply to income and production.

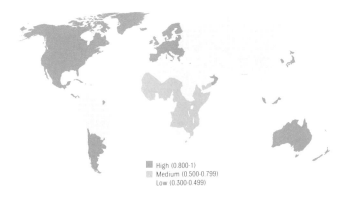

High (0.800-1)
Medium (0.500-0.799)
Low (0.300-0.499)

Above: The Human Development Index (HDI) measures GDP, life expectancy, and educational attainment, along with other socio-economic factors, to reveal the inequalities between the developing and the developed world

In his work on famine, Sen emphasises that poverty and hunger are not always the result of shortages of food through a failure of production, but can be due to a failure of distribution. Social mechanisms, rather than resource scarcity or overpopulation, may be the primary obstacle to provisioning.

At the core of Sen's critique of traditional approaches is the mainstream emphasis on individual rationality. He rejects the rationality assumption and has shown its weaknesses in several significant papers. Strict adherence to the rationality principle would make humans 'rational fools', and such an approach ignores the necessity of what Adam Smith, in his *Theory of Moral Sentiments* (1759), called 'sympathy' (empathy in current terminology) for a stable social and economic order. At the heart of Sen's work is his call for ethics to be regarded as an integral part of economics.

Development Economics

Glossary

Business cycle: Repetitive cycles of economic expansion and contraction.

Capital: Money capital finances investment; industrial capital or capital goods are produced by means of production such as machines or tools, used to produce commodities for sale in a market.

Capital accumulation: Investment or economic growth.

Classical Economics: A deductive approach to economic analysis, often accompanied by historical and empirical material.

Deficit: An excess of liabilities over assets, of losses over profits, or of expenditure over income.

Deregulation: The reduction of government's role in controlling markets, which leads to freer markets.

Economic growth rate: The annual percentage rate of change in the Gross Domestic Product.

Fiscal policy: Government spending and taxing for the specific purpose of stabilising the economy.

Free trade: International trade left to its natural course without tariffs, quotas or other restrictions.

General economic equilibrium: A branch of theoretical microeconomics that seeks to explain production, consumption, and prices in a whole economy, rather than in just one market.

Gross Domestic Product (GDP): Total money value of final goods and services produced in a year, measured in terms of the residents of a nation rather than its citizenry.

HDI Index: The Human Development Index – a comparative measure of life expectancy, literacy, education and standards of living for countries worldwide.

Inflation: Persistent increase in the average level of prices, or general price level.

Input–output tables: Tables that indicate how much each industry requires of the production of each other industry in order to produce each dollar of its own output.

Institutional economics: US-based historical and evolutionary approach to economics associated with Thorstein Veblen.

Interventionism: A term used to describe activity undertaken by a central government to affect a country's economy in an attempt to increase economic growth and/or standards of living.

Laissez-faire: The doctrine that a government should not interfere with business and economic affairs.

Macroeconomics: Analysis of a country's economic activity as a whole; the theory of aggregate output, employment, and the price level.

Marginal utility: The additional satisfaction resulting from the consumption of one additional unit of a specific good or service.

Microeconomics: Analysis of the economic behaviour of individual households and firms interacting through markets; the theory of value and distribution.

Monetary policy: Actions taken by the Central Bank to influence the money supply or interest rates. Monetary policy is a tool by which government can influence the economy by affecting interest rates.

Monetarism: The school of thought that maintains that money supply is the chief determinant of economic activity and that argues that inflation is best controlled by limiting the supply of money circulating in an economy.

Monopoly: Market characterised by absolute control of all sales and distribution in the market by one firm, allowing the firm to sell at a higher price than the societally optimal price.

Multiplier: Economic feedback mechanism that amplifies any change in autonomous spending.

National income: Total income of a country measured as the sum of wages, interest, profits and rents in one year.

Neoclassical economics: An approach to economics that considers prices to be determined by an equilibrium of supply and demand; stresses individual rationality as maximisation of utility or profit.

Oligopoly: A market characterised by a few large producers who often act together to control the supply of a particular good and its market price.

Opportunity costs: The opportunity cost of using resources in one way is the value that could have been produced if the resources were used in the best alternative way.

Partial equilibrium: A branch of microeconomics that views firms and markets in isolation, holding all other factors in other markets constant.

Perfect competition: An idealised market environment in which every market participant is too small, and there are so many of them, that none can affect the market price by acting on its own. Includes other assumptions such as perfectly flexible prices, perfect mobility of land, labour, and capital, perfect knowledge, etc.

Planned economy: An economic system in which a single agency makes all decisions about the production and allocation of goods and services.

Privatisation: The transfer of government-owned or government-run companies to the private sector, usually by selling them.

Profit: Total revenue minus total costs.

Recession: A temporary downturn in economic activity, usually indicated by two consecutive quarters of a falling GDP.

Specie: A commodity metal, historically gold and silver, backing money or currency.

Stagflation: A period of slow economic growth and high unemployment with rising prices.

Subsistence economy: Referring to production at a level sufficient only for one's own use, without any surplus for trade.

Supply-side economics: A theory of economics that reductions in tax rates will stimulate investment and in turn will benefit the entire society.

Surplus funds: Cash flow available after payment of taxes in a project.

Index

For main economist entries see contents page. References to economists are given only where mentioned other than their main entry.